D0857635

Language Games to Play with Your Child

Enhancing Communication from Infancy through Late Childhood

New and Revised Edition

Also by Allyssa McCabe (with Carole Peterson)

Developmental Psycholinguistics: Three Ways of Looking at a Child's Narrative

Developing Narrative Structure

Language Games to Play with Your Child

Enhancing Communication from Infancy through Late Childhood

New and Revised Edition

Allyssa McCabe, Ph.D.

 **INSIGHT BOOKS**

Plenum Press • New York and London

Library of Congress Cataloging-in-Publication Data

McCabe, Allyssa.
    Language games to play with your child : enhancing communication
from infancy through late childhood / Allyssa McCabe. -- New and
revised ed.
        p.   cm.
    Includes bibliographical references and index.
    ISBN 0-306-44320-1
    1. Children--Language. 2. Literary recreations. 3. Language
acquisition.   I. Title.
LB1139.L3M26   1992
372.6--dc20   92-19084
                                                                    CIP

This new and revised edition has been updated from the original version,
which was published in 1987 by Ballantine Books.

ISBN 0-306-44320-1

© 1992, 1987 Allyssa McCabe
Insight Books is a division of Plenum Publishing Corporation
233 Spring Street, New York, N.Y. 10013

An Insight Book

Printed in the United States of America

For Jessamyn and Nicholas

For Jessamyn and Nicholas

Preface to the New and Revised Edition

Since the first edition of this book was published in 1987, much exciting research has been done in the field of child language. More researchers subscribe to the social interactionist theory of language, the theory of language development on which this book is based. We now know substantially more than we did before about how to facilitate the language development of children.

First, I have completed a study examining the way that parents interview their children about past events. For about five years, Carole Peterson and I have recorded and transcribed conversations in ten families. At the outset of our study the children were just two years old; now they are almost seven. We know which children tell good stories and which don't, and how their parents contributed to their storytelling abilities. We no longer have to rely on hunches about the best way to talk to a child.

Second, Catherine Snow, who is largely responsible for devising the social interactionist theory of language development, and David Dickinson have begun to have results from their study of the kinds of language experiences low-income children have at home and at school. They have followed more than eighty low-income children from the age of three years; those children are now almost six. Again, Snow and Dickinson now are beginning to see which children are advanced in terms of many different language skills, including early forms of reading and writing. They also know what kinds of language from teachers and parents have helped advance children along the way.

One theme emerging from the Snow-Dickinson study, as well as from other studies, is that a child's ability to talk is related in specific ways to his or her ability to read and write. Reading and writing are not simply skills one learns in school. In many ways, children have been preparing to read and write for years before they even enter school.

Throughout this edition, I have added games and advice based on the results of a number of interesting projects by researchers working on such diverse topics as bilingualism, reading, and metaphor in laboratories all over North America. In fact, the main reason I revised the book was to make that information available to parents.

On the strength of such studies, I have added two new games: What Did You Say, Dear? and Explanations. What Did You Say, Dear? picks up on the fact that parents who truly try to communicate with their children let the children know when they have not made their point. When both parents and children continue to make the effort, communication is eventually achieved and, over time, the children become more adept at communicating in the first place. Explanations highlights a most important game some parents play with children, a game whose impact on language development, thinking, and understanding of social and emotional issues cannot be underestimated.

Another reason for publishing a revision at this time is that speech pathologists and other professionals who work with children have become much more precise in diagnosing learning disabilities that are fundamentally problems in language development. These professionals attempt to diagnose problems as early as possible and to involve parents in attempting to treat their children. I hope that this book will prove useful for those parents and children who are struggling with language development, as well as for those who are having an easier time. Many researchers agree that parents are not to blame for the difficulty their children may have in mastering language. Still, parents can begin to try to improve their children's language skills by talking to them in ways described in this book. In fact, the same researchers who agree that parents of children with language delay did not cause that delay also argue that without special help the impairment will continue. In other words, children who are not naturally adept at picking up language need even more practice playing language games of the sort I will describe than children who seem to pick up language normally.

General features of these language games include the following: (1) they playfully draw children's attention to a number of rules of language; (2) they point out situations such as mealtimes and book-reading in which conversations between adults and children are appropriate and, I hope, make adults aware of the fact that conversations with their children are appropriate and desirable in almost *any situation*, for example, while grocery shopping or waiting in the doctor's office; and (3) they give children a lot of practice producing language. These are the features of interventions for language delay that seem most important.

A third reason for revising this book is the increased attention developmental psychologists, educators, and parents are directing at the process of language development. We have come a long way from the old, abusive maxim that children should be seen and not heard. Many parents realize that it is important that children be encouraged to talk. Parents are anxious not to have the kinds of problems communicating with their children that they themselves may have had with their own parents.

One sign of such increased interest is that since the first edition of this book was published, articles on language development inspired by the book have been published in such national magazines as *Parents, Working Mother, Child,* and *American Baby.* I have been a guest on a variety of television and radio programs. With more babies being born to parents who are accustomed to being

well informed about everything from clapboard siding to choles-
terol, it is perhaps natural that such parents would seek information about something they find themselves doing a lot of—namely,
talking to their children.

Another very important phenomenon is the Whole Language
Movement in educational circles. More and more reading teachers
are moving away from skills drills and turning to an approach to
instruction that is based on language development research and
that recognizes the importance of always using language com-
municatively.

Such teachers believe children are eager to learn anything
they need to learn in order to communicate with people around
them, while those same children understandably may tune out
what seem to be meaningless repetitions of fragments of language.
Some teachers also emphasize the importance of reading classic
children's fiction instead of, or at least in addition to, basal readers,
which base selections primarily on the predictability of their vocabulary. A good story will kindle children's interest in mastering
even somewhat difficult vocabulary, while predictable vocabulary
will not spark children's interest in a banal story.

Yet despite the growing awareness that talking to children is
a good thing to do and despite the fact that such information
exists, specific information about *how* to talk to children is not
readily available. Popular parenting books still are likely to devote
most of their space to advice on physical, cognitive, and social
development of children and to give only a page or two at most to
considering language development. This book is intended to fill
that gap.

Language development is not only as important as cognitive
and social-emotional development in children; it is the most important means by which both are achieved after the age of two
years. At this age, children begin to talk out loud in order to think
about what they are going to do next. Parents can begin to give
children words to express feelings and resolve fights. Parents can
explain their own feelings and behaviors and reasons for rules to

their children. The more children can talk, the better they will be able to think and to get along with parents, peers, and siblings.

While all kinds of language games can be fun, the ones I have collected here are vital. They will and perhaps should seem almost frivolous at first. They need to be played for fun. Yet all are also nutritious.

When the first edition of this book was published, my children were five years younger. After five additional years of "field-testing" these games, I am more confident than ever of their importance and usefulness. As they have grown older, my children have taken the initiative in playing many of these games. We tell Dream Reports at breakfast and narratives about our day at dinner (see Tell a Story to Get a Story). My son suggests that we play What If? or think up an alphabet of pastas or birds or flowers every time we ride in the car. My daughter enjoys games of The Rain Stays Mainly on the Plain and Wonderful Willowy Words and applies her poetic abilities in the entertaining, well-developed stories she is always telling and writing at home and at school. Children who can talk well are a joy to talk with.

I would like to thank Charlie Cuneo for his editing, support, and sense of humor throughout this project.

Reference

Snow, C. E. and Dickinson, D. K. (1991, April). The Social Prerequisites of Literary Development: Home and School Experiences of Pre-school-aged Children from Low-income Families. A Symposium Presented at the Annual Meetings of the American Educational Research Association, Chicago, Illinois.

Preface to the First Edition

This book provides over a hundred ways to have fun with your child by playing language games with him. But language games are much more than just fun—they are a wonderful way to develop your child's language, his ability to think and to read, as well as his emotions and his relationship with you. Language, thought, and emotions are completely intertwined in childhood. When something is really wrong with a child, it is often hard to tell whether the fundamental problem is an emotional one that has triggered difficulty in learning or whether it is a learning disorder that has triggered emotional problems. On the brighter side, when my daughter plays one of my favorite language games, Once Upon a Time, she tells me things that are bothering her at the same time that she is improving her ability to tell a well-structured story. Since one of the things she is worrying about is her fear of fierce and powerful giants (her parents?), I have heard dozens of tales about fierce Tyrannosaurus Rexes who scare little girl dolphins but turn out not to be so bad, and each such story is better structured than the last.

WHAT IS A LANGUAGE GAME?

A language game is a spoken routine for two or more players, meant to be repeated many times. Such repetition engenders a comforting set of expectations in your child and yourself. To play a favorite language game is to achieve instant understanding between you and your child. You both know where you are. You both have been here before, and you both like it.

I have borrowed the idea of "language games" from the European philosopher, Ludwig Wittgenstein. Although I think he would approve of my use of the term, I admittedly have made liberal use of it.

Language games are set apart from ordinary conversation with children in that they generally have special rules and are meant to be repeated. In contrast, ordinary conversation with children is a set of one-shot exchanges in which your focus is on the topic: What is the child being asked to do? Which particular toy is being discussed? Who is sick?

In a language game, your focus is on the form of the spoken exchange. *What* is said is less important than *how* it is said. The rules must be followed.

WHY PLAY LANGUAGE GAMES?

Play language games because they are fun. In fact, there is no better fun than communication with your child. Talking to your child is the key to a good emotional relationship with him. Language games will also give your child the vocabulary to articulate his emotions so that he need not resort to acting them out.

Play language games with your child because they will help him develop language and thought. To say what you mean is to think clearly. In the course of playing the language games I have included here, your child will develop his ability to say what he means to say, to express himself clearly. A child who cannot express himself clearly will often be frustrated. He will not get what he wants or be able to play with other children well, and he may lash out aggressively in his frustration. Children who lag behind their peers intellectually often develop behavior problems.

Play language games with your child because language development is the foundation for developing the ability to read. Problems in reading are often problems in language development. Success in language development is a prerequisite for success in reading. The language games I have chosen for younger children are intended to develop the particular skills necessary for reading. Even more important, they are intended to instill a love of language and a deep and abiding interest in the way things are said, both of which distinguish a good from a mediocre or poor reader.

Although your child will acquire language as these games are played, play these games for fun, not specifically for the purpose of instruction. Remember, this is *not* a book on how to teach your children language. Children do not need to be *taught* language, strictly speaking. In fact, teaching language may have the opposite effect from the one parents intend. A study by Katherine Nelson showed that when mothers rewarded their children for correct pronunciation and punished them for bad, the children developed language more slowly than children whose mothers were more tolerant and more interested in what their children were saying rather than how they were saying it. Parental anxiety about proper pronunciation has been pointed out as one reason some children stutter. Enjoy your child's bungles instead of worrying about them. A good conversation at any age usually involves a certain amount of forgiveness and overlooking of faults. I hope this book will prompt conversation between parents and children, while making parents more aware of the blossoming of language that begins by an infant "practicing vowels" with his very first cry.

WHEN SHOULD LANGUAGE GAMES BE PLAYED?

Some language games take minutes to play, some can take hours. There is usually no fixed amount of time required to play a game. How long you play will depend on the nature of the game and the age and mood of your child. Never try to continue a game past the point at which your child is interested in it. Even before children are old enough to tell you outright what they think about the games, they will tell you by their attention or lack of it. A child who is interested in a game will look at you and vocalize back; a child who is not ready to play a particular game or who is too old for a game will ignore you.

If your child does not respond to a certain game, try another one. Try the same game another time, when he is in a better mood—rested, well fed, and smiling. Some language games are just for fun and may not be to every child's taste. If you try to play one of these games with your child a dozen times with no response, drop it for the time being. Try it again when he is older. I indicate at the end of each introductory section which games are a must for each age group because of the crucial role they play in developing language skills. Keep on trying to play these games with your child. Again, familiarity breeds delight for most children.

WHERE SHOULD LANGUAGE GAMES BE PLAYED?

Most language games can be played anywhere—at home, in the car, in the supermarket. Most language games require nothing more than two voices: yours and your child's. For this reason, good times to play language games are times when you and your child are traveling or waiting for something—an airplane to land, a doctor's appointment, a meal at a restaurant, a clerk at a department store. A good language game can turn a trying time into fun. The language games in this book that do require props require things that you are likely to have available.

HOW IS THIS BOOK STRUCTURED?

The first chapter is an overview of language development, along with an introduction to the general theories of development upon which I draw. The rest of the book is divided into sections based loosely on the age at which you should begin to play certain language games. At the beginning of each section, I have written an essay about the developmental issues your child will face at the age in question. First, I give information regarding a child's general language development. Because I do not think that children develop language in a vacuum, I talk about what parents should be doing as I discuss what children should be doing at each particular age. Next, I present information about individual differences in language development during each age range. You cannot talk well to a child unless you know what kind of a child you are talking to, so I present information about the general emotional, cognitive, perceptual, and physical development in which language development is embedded. Throughout the essay, I refer to the games in the section relevant to developmental issues being discussed. At the end of each developmental essay, I tell you which games are essential for development and which are just for fun.

HOW SHOULD YOU
USE THIS BOOK?

There are a number of ways to use this book. Some people will buy it and read only the section that fits the age of their child. That is okay. However, it would be better if you read through the book prior to the section that fits the age of your child. I introduce language games as soon as they are capable of being enjoyed. In no sense should games be abandoned at the end of the age range in which they are first described. In other words, if you read only the games in the age range of your child, you will miss out on a number of games he might enjoy that are introduced in earlier sections. You might also read ahead. Some children may enjoy language games intended for older children. A child's stage of language development is far more important than his age in determining what language games he will enjoy playing. Normal children vary quite a bit in how rapidly they acquire language.

WHO SHOULD USE THIS BOOK?

Parents, stepparents, teachers, anyone who will be talking to children and feels a little rusty at it.

Talking to children is a lot like dancing. Some of us are naturally graceful partners. Others are awkward and clumsy; we talk too loudly or too forcefully, at too high or too low a level for the child we are addressing.

Even people who are very good at talking to children most of the time could use some new ideas. Mothers who stay at home with their children all day long may find their conversation falling into some predictable ruts. Parents who work outside the house may have high hopes of fantastic conversation with their children at the end of the day, yet be a little short of the energy required to invent a good exchange. They may also find it a little disconcerting to shift from talking to highly verbal adults all day to talking to their little verbal fledgling at night. Teachers could adapt some of the games in this book for use in the classroom. My hope is that this book will provide some ideas for all of these people.

This book is also intended for professionals who work with children but may not have their own, for people who find themselves stepparents overnight, for relatives who do not get much chance to see their little kin. People who do not talk easily to children usually know they don't. I have heard them nervously confess as much. Unfortunately, the consequences of an inability to talk to children can be disastrous if that person is a stepparent, for example. Or a biological parent, for that matter, who feels that he is unable to communicate with his children. Or any relative. Or a teacher.

Fortunately, like dancing, talking to children can be an acquired skill. This book is designed to help you learn it. Although it is geared primarily for parents who know their children well, the book also may prove useful to people who want to know how to talk to children they do not know well.

There is really nothing mysterious about an ability to speak to children you have just met. The so-called natural talent for this boils down to a few simple rules. The first rule is do not come on too strong. Greet a child, then talk to that child's parent. Children are often naturally shy when they meet strangers. These days, many children are even specifically coached not to talk to strangers. Let the child see you talking to the parent and receiving his or her approval first. If the child looks at you, smile, but don't push. Most children will eventually make an overture to you once they have had time to decide you are safe. Let them come to you.

For young children, rule two is be ready to abandon your conversation with other adults when a child does approach you. It takes a while for children to understand about waiting for their turn in the conversation. So you have to be willing to be interrupted to respond to them. You cannot call the shots with young children and expect to communicate successfully with them. I have seen some people make a big push to talk to a young child at first. The child typically hides behind his parent's leg. The person eventually quits trying to talk to the child after several hearty questions are ignored and turns his attention to the child's parent. Then when the child does make some overture, asking if the person wants to see a toy, for instance, the person either ignores the child and continues talking to the parent or says, "Not right now. I'm in the middle of something. Just a minute." Needless to say, when the person gets around to trying to talk to the child again, the child either has fled or again retreated into silence. That person has just blown a meeting with the child twice. It will be hard to get on the right track after this, particularly if the person decides either that the child is a brat or that he himself is hopeless at talking to children.

WHO AM I?

As an undergraduate at Oberlin College, I majored both in English and psychology. My interest in English has never waned and is reflected in this book perhaps as strongly in some ways as is my interest in psychology. I received my Ph.D. in psychology from the University of Virginia in 1980. Since that time, I have taught developmental, cognitive, language, and other psychology courses at several institutions, including Harvard University and Tufts University. I have done research on a number of topics in language development and published articles in the *Journal of Child Language, Developmental Psychology*, and *Journal of Psycholinguistic Research*. With Carole Peterson, I published *Developmental Psycholinguistics: Three Ways of Looking at a Child's Narrative* and *Developing Narrative Structures*. These books examined the structure of children's personal narratives, something I have drawn on in this present book.

For my research, I trained dozens of undergraduates to talk to children of all ages, normal and delinquent. Many of these undergraduates swore to me that they had not talked to a child since their younger sibling was born years ago. They all succeeded in learning how to talk to children quite well.

So much for me professionally. I am also the mother of two children. When my eldest child, my daughter, was born, so was the idea for this book. I wanted to convert what I knew as a professional into something I could use as a mother. I knew that buried in tables of numbers to the tenth decimal point and in elegant jargon of four and five syllables lay information that would be of use to me when I came home very tired, my brain feeling like a heap of sawdust, after a long day's work. I wanted to share some much touted "quality time" with my little daughter. But I needed a list of ideas for how to talk to her to make up for a lack of sleep, which had eroded my imagination, my energy, and my patience.

I plowed through all my scholarly data, journals, and books and thought about it for a while. Here is the result. I hope you, too, will find it useful.

Contents

Introduction

HOW DOES YOUR CHILD LEARN TO TALK?

Language development is like a French braid. New abilities are picked up like strands as the child goes along, and these abilities are worked into the design of previously acquired abilities, which also continue to develop. The strands in question are pronunciation, vocabulary, sentence construction, connected discourse such as narratives, reading, and writing. In other words, as I describe the general course of language development here, understand that the emerging abilities highlighted at any particular age have been developing before the age described and will, with a few exceptions, continue to develop for a very long time. Cooing and babbling emerge and fade relatively rapidly, but children work on the pronunciation of words for seven or eight years. They also work on developing understanding and production of complex sentences for at least as long. Nine-year-olds are still improving the narratives they tell. It takes ten years or so to become a truly proficient reader. It may take twenty or thirty years to really learn to write. We build our vocabularies throughout our whole lives.

A newborn baby is just waking up. The first six months of life is, in a way, a period of time devoted to waking up, literally and figuratively, in terms of language development. Newborns sleep a lot. They do not have any language per se. But they do cry from birth on, and this crying strengthens their vocal cords and lungs. At about one month, infants begin to coo, which is much more pleasant, and parents often coo back. Cooing is largely comprised of vowel-like sounds. Again, cooing is not really language, but, like crying, it prompts communication with parents, and it is vocalizing: two prerequisites for language.

At six months, your child will be getting organized to speak. She will begin to babble, producing consonants for the first time. To start with, she mostly will babble a few syllables, like mamamamamama or babababababa. But by the time she is about ten months old, she will be babbling English. Really. She will not babble the way a baby whose parents speak Chinese or Russian will babble. Babbling is simply playing with sounds at first, but by the time she is one, your child may have developed a babble-word or two, namely, a regular sound that she makes in predictable situations. You will have imitated your child almost from birth, and now she will begin to imitate you.

From twelve to eighteen months is a time of getting up and ready for real language. Your child will work very hard to build a rather limited vocabulary. She will use one word at a time, but mean that word to stand for a sentence of thought. She will get maximum use out of her limited vocabulary by overgeneralizing her words, using a word she knows to refer to an object that is new to her or for which she does not have the correct name.

Your child will be taking off talking at eighteen months. Her vocabulary will explode. She will add many new words almost without effort, quite a contrast to her laborious word-by-word efforts earlier on. This vocabulary learning will continue throughout her life. Your child will also begin to combine words. These combinations make it clear that she is not simply imitating you. For example, my little eighteen-month-old daughter said, "Byebye hot" when her father covered the barbeque grill that she had been instructed was quite hot. We had said nothing of the sort for her to copy.

Two-year-olds have a bad reputation, a reputation that they

are negative, that they reject most suggestions you make. This reputation is, unfortunately, well deserved. But from the point of view of language development, two-year-olds are also fun. From two to three, your child will be working on several new aspects of language, in addition to continued attention to pronunciation and vocabulary building. One of the most exciting new things is genuine conversational turn-taking. Of course, you may have exchanged coos and babbling for almost a year, but now your child can actually talk back and forth with you. For example, when my husband and I told our daughter that we had to go somewhere and leave her with a babysitter, she regularly replied, "Maybe I cry." At least now we could talk about the situation. Other new abilities include an ability to discuss abstract things, like feelings, with lengthening sentences. My daughter came up with the following discourse when she was two and a half: "I saw the sun. He come to me like a carriage. He is trying to *catch* me."Incidentally, most accounts of language development stop here at two years. Oh, the "experts" may toss off a few lines about older children. But it is at least in part to correct the standard idea that all of language is learned by age two that I set out to write this account.

Three-year-olds enter the phase I describe as sleep-talking. I give it this name for the charmingly unself-conscious way that children at this age think aloud. Much of my discussion of preschool language development concerns this interaction with preschool thought. Of course, preschoolers accomplish several purely linguistic feats. For one thing, they systematically add endings to words, saying "dogs" when there is more than one dog, "Daddy's" when pointing to a placemat. They are more systematic than adults are in this respect. A three-year-old will overdo the application of these endings, saying "That's mines," as well as "That's Daddy's."

Three- and four-year-olds will tell narratives about what happens to them, but they often do so in a chaotic fashion, leaping back and forth in time to give you a few of the important events that made up one of their experiences. They even may leave out altogether some very important events.

Five-year-olds generally have developed enough skill in narrating to tell you a series of events in the order in which they happened. However, they tend to tell cliffhanger narratives that leave you hanging at the main event of the story.

Six-year-olds have mastered the rudiments of telling a good narrative. They begin by orienting their listener to the context of their narrative, namely, who was involved and where and when something happened. They go on to give the series of events that culminated in the high point of the story for them, and they let you know what that high point was in no uncertain terms. Then they go on to let you know how things worked out. A classic narrative. Of course, they will continue to improve their narrative style for a while, but it is well in place at age six.

The five- to seven-year-old child is in transition from babyhood to a stage where much more will be expected of her in every way. Somewhere during this time, in a variety of ways, she will display a readiness to learn how to read, in addition to learning how to tell a good oral narrative. Many children begin to decode words at this time. A child may become quite cocky about her newfound abilities. She will be in kindergarten, then first grade, during this time, getting her feet wet in school.

A seven- to nine-year-old child is steeped in all sorts of rules, from those involved in learning how to read to rules for solid citizenship among her peers. She has become society's child. The primary focus of language development during these years is reading, and a child will spend her time at age seven trying to decipher simple words. By age eight or nine, she will be a much more fluent reader, and her attention will shift from figuring out how to read individual words to trying to understand the meaning of what she reads.

While she has been learning how to read, your child has also been working on writing skills, mastering the letters of the alphabet, putting together words in sentences, maybe even occasionally writing a story. At nine, with reading well in place, writing becomes the language skill to focus on. Your child at first will show little regard for her audience, but with time she increasingly will think about that audience. At first, her written sentences will be considerably simpler than her spoken ones, but this eventually reverses. Finally, she will spend a lot of time at school mastering new genres of writing, the most important of which is the report. From now on, in her writing, your child increasingly will differentiate herself from her peers. Of course, she may dress exactly like her best friend, but when it comes to writing, individual differences begin to overwhelm developmental ones. Your child will become a real character in her writing.

Children do not acquire language in a smooth, forward path of progress. Instead, they develop it in fits and starts. For example, today they will seem to have completely forgotten the names of those objects they named so clearly yesterday. Or they will seem to have mastered words like "went" or "ran," and then for the next several months you will hear them saying "goed" or "runned." This is not a book that will tell you how to prevent what seems to be such backsliding. In fact, I hope this book will make you appreciate and even enjoy such "mistakes." The fact that children predictably go through a stage when they say "goed" and "comed" shows that children do not simply imitate their parents speech. Children experiment, generalize, and generally contribute a great deal to their own language development.

INDIVIDUAL DIFFERENCES

While these are the general trends in developing language, it is important to recognize that there are a great many individual differences at every stage of this development. There are considerable differences in the rate at which children progress, as well as stylistic differences all along the line. Some babies cry almost continuously, some rarely cry. Some cry in a strident, irritating manner, some cry rather more gently most of the time. Some babies coo in a singsong fashion, others coo in squeaks and grunts with a few raspberries thrown in. Some coo a lot, some only a little. Some take turns cooing, others crow to themselves. Some children babble early on and a lot. Some children never babble at all. Some children have their first recognizable word at ten months, some not until two and a half. When older, some children become great storytellers, expanding at length on their experiences. Other children summarize what happens to them in a sentence or two.

When children start developing words, there is a great deal of variation in their method of language learning. Some imitate their parents a lot, replaying whole chunks of adults' speech. These are the children who, at their parents' slightest prompting, will go into whole routines of songs when they are only two years old. Other children resist immediate imitation of adults, preferring to name things when they want to and seldom imitating things to oblige their parents. When they are older, some children learn to read by paying meticulous attention to the specific words of a text, while others abandon such concern for accuracy in a competing concern to keep up the momentum of a text that is so crucial for understanding it.

All these variations are normal. We know of no simple connection between intelligence and these stylistic differences in form and method of language learning. Virtually all children end up mastering their native language. Appreciate your child's individuality! Do not fret about it.

THE CONTEXT OF LANGUAGE DEVELOPMENT

Language development is embedded in the midst of the development of other aspects of personality. There are many different accounts of emotional development, but none is as accurate, useful, and well grounded in observational research as the Attachment Theory developed by John Bowlby and Mary Ainsworth. My account of emotional development is based largely on Bowlby and Ainsworth's ideas, especially in the chapters "Birth to Six Months," "Six to Twelve Months," "Twelve to Eighteen Months," "Eighteen Months to Two Years," and "Preschool: Three to Five Years." The giant in cognitive development theory is still Jean

Piaget, even though many subsequent researchers have confirmed, extended, or corrected his ideas. My discussions of cognitive development will reflect Piaget, as well as these subsequent researchers. In the first two years of a child's life, perceptual and physical abilities are developing dramatically, and I draw my discussion of these developments from what is generally known about them in the field of psychology.

WHY DOES YOUR CHILD LEARN TO TALK?

Children develop language by talking with adults, primarily their parents. They are born with special anatomical features that enable them to acquire language, but that is not sufficient to achieve the enormously complex task of language acquisition. Social interaction with adults is essential. This theory of how language is acquired was launched in 1972, when Catherine Snow published an article examining various aspects of the special way in which adults talk to infants. Adults produce simpler, more redundant, less confusing speech to two-year-olds than to ten-year-olds, for example. Thus children who are in the process of learning language have available to them language that is excellently suited for just that.

This balanced view of the contributions of both nature and nurture to the language acquisition process replaces older theories that emphasized either one or the other source. Until 1957, psychologists believed that children learned language in the same way that rats learned to press bars. That is, they assumed that if children were rewarded for better and better attempts to produce a word correctly and were ignored or punished whenever they made sounds that were not wordlike, then the children would eventually produce words. Just like rats. Rats are easy to study. They stay in cages and do not cry and can be starved to motivate them to learn faster. Since most psychologists believed that children learned in the same way as rats, there seemed to be little reason to study children. Much information was collected about the best way to reward your child and about the relative merits of reward and punishment based largely on studies of rats.

In 1957, Noam Chomsky changed all this by publishing *Aspects of the Theory of Syntax*. This book was revolutionary in many ways, but one of the most important was its view that children were not "taught" their native language. Chomsky instead considered children to be biologically programmed to acquire language with even minimal exposure to speaking adults. He thought that as children's brains developed, so would their language. Research in the 1960s and early 1970s focused almost exclusively on chronicling the developmental accomplishments of children and ignored the role of parents. You could get the idea from reading most of the studies published at this time that children acquired language in an empty room.

Somewhere along the line, people decided that it was very bad to talk babytalk to a child. Whenever I talk about language development, I meet up with people who claim that they do not talk any differently to their children than to adults. Fortunately, people do not always act the way they say they do. After rather violently claiming that she never "talked down to children at any age," one grandmother turned around and began playing the Oh, You Beautiful Baby game with an infant. The infant responded with a lovely cooing song. If you really do talk to children no differently than you talk to adults, either you are underestimating the adults or overestimating the children.

As I have said, babytalk meets the needs of children just learning how to talk by providing language that is simple enough and related enough to the child's focus of attention that the child can connect words with things. Perhaps babytalk's bad reputation stems from incidents where adults inappropriately use babytalk to children much farther along in the language-learning process. In any case, this book attempts to specify what aspects of babytalk have been demonstrated to facilitate language development and how adults' talk to children optimally should change as the children grow older.

Children acquire much of their language by playing language

games with adults. Recent research has turned up a number of language games that many (but not all) parents play with their children, and some of these will be included here. Psychologists working in the laboratory have realized that they can get children to talk more to them by devising tests of language skills that are in the form of games, and some of these also will be included here. I have included some original language games invented by myself or by my friends. Some of the games will be familiar to you, although I have tried to include some new twists to them. Some of the games almost certainly will be new to you, and I hope they are as enjoyable as the old standbys. I have enjoyed playing all these games myself with many children. I hope that the spirit of the book inspires you and your children to create your own language games.

✳ 1 ✳

Birth to Six Months

"She's just starting to talk now," many parents say about their one-year-old toddler. But contrary to popular opinion, language development really begins at birth, or even before; the games in this section will facilitate language learning.

Your newborn's vocalizing is pretty much limited for about a month to crying. But did you realize that newborn crying has been recorded as containing at least eight different speech sounds, mostly vowels? Specifically, newborn infants can produce the vowels in the following words: "fat," "fit," "set," "food," "up." They can also produce an *h* and an *l* and something known as a glottal stop, which is similar to the *h* sound in English. Not all infants produce all these speech sounds. Most infants tend, in fact, to prefer the "aahhh" sound. Surprisingly, infants do practice their vowel sounds while crying.

More important, infants communicate with their crying. Your infant cries because something is wrong; crying is her only means of telling you about it. You may worry about spoiling your child by paying attention to her crying, but this is not something you should be concerned about. Research indicates that prompt attention to your infant's cries is the basis for the first successful communication between you and will result in her crying less often by the time she is one year old. Parents who are unresponsive to their infant's crying in this early time produce an infant who cries more frequently later on. In other words, crying is not a nasty habit to be broken. It is a signal to you that your child needs something.

By the way, one of the most effective means of quieting a crying baby is to talk to her. And talking to your child in a high-pitched voice is the best way of getting her to smile even when she is only two weeks old.

At about one month, your infant will begin more pleasant vocalizing, namely cooing, which sounds like singing and is often accompanied by smiling. This is the time that you can begin to play real language games. As I point out in Oh, You Beautiful Baby, you can encourage your child to coo more frequently by responding to her.

Infants have different styles of cooing. Some infants coo frequently. Some rarely do. Some coo for long periods of time. Others coo for shorter times. My daughter treated us to lengthy coo songs. I was very much surprised by my son's style of cooing, which was one that sounded more like a series of grunts and squeaks, which he punctuated at odd moments by blowing raspberries. I enjoyed both styles tremendously.

Infants also differ in terms of how much they cry. Some cry rarely and for short periods of time. Others cry virtually their entire first year. Children are born with different temperaments. My sympathies are with those parents whose babies cry all the time.

Premature infants may cry in a way that is particularly disturbing to adults. They will not coo as soon after birth as full-term infants.

Language unfolds amid development in a number of other areas. Language affects and, in turn, is affected by such changes. In fact, you cannot really talk about development in one area without talking about development in other areas. As I have been implying already in this discussion, the most important area of simultaneous development is that of emotions.

Mary Ainsworth defines attachment as "an affectional tie that one person forms to another specific person, binding them together in space and enduring over time." Infants develop nothing less important than the capacity to love another human being during the first couple of years of their lives. They need concentrated interaction with one or two adults in order to form the capacity to love. A whole host of adult caretakers impersonally taking charge of the child's physical needs will not be able to nurture this basic human need for personal attention, for specific love.

Attachment is forged by contact between one particular adult and one particular child, by their exchange of gazes and smiles, and by the adult responding to the child's crying and cooing at this time. The child is not attached to a biological parent at birth. In fact, attachment has nothing to do with shared genes. Too many parents have abandoned or ignored their children, banking on their blood relationship for future love. They have been disappointed. Attachment must be earned by parents in the sense that they must interact with the child in order for the child to become attached to them. While taking care of your child's needs is of paramount importance in forming her attachment to you, playful interaction encourages the development of language and communication, and may affect the quality of your relationship.

For the first three months, your child will smile at you, be comforted by your high-pitched voice, and exchange coos with you. But she will do just the same thing with the strange woman who is standing ahead of you in the grocery line. In other words, your child does not really single you out for special attention during this time. Your life is utterly changed by her. You are a zombie from lack of sleep because of getting up in the night to comfort her. You think she is the only perfect baby in the world. Yet she is promiscuous with her signals for affection. She is in the first phase of emotional development, the phase of undiscriminating social responsiveness.

Then at about four months, your child will change. Your interaction with her, verbal and otherwise, will pay off. She will recognize your face and give you smiles more readily than she will give those with whom she has not interacted as much. She will be more easily comforted by you and your spouse than by others. She will have entered a new phase of emotional development, the phase known as discriminating social responsiveness.

Four months is also the time of dramatic cognitive development. Up until this time, your child has been capable of reflex actions such as grasping your finger. You can play with your newborn's reflexes. See how much you can tug while she is grasping your finger. Or try tickling her feet to see her fan her toes upward before she goes into the downward curl characteristic of adults. Those reflex actions either disappear or adapt somewhat to deal with new situations.

At four months, your infant will become very interested in the world around her. Before, when you played with her, she showed no interest in the toys you may have tried to offer her. But now she actively plays with toys, grasping them, shaking them, putting them in her mouth. In short, she will do everything she is capable of doing with whatever catches her attention.

According to Piaget, infants think in a sensorimotor way. In other words, your child thinks by looking and listening to things and by manipulating them. You watch her "think" as you watch her play. Do not give her anything that you do not want her to think about by touching. I have seen too many attractive, expensive toys that are meant only to be watched, not touched. These are torture to young infants. Truly, I once saw a five-month-old boy become hysterical because he was understandably prevented from touching his Christmas present, which was a colorful mechanical train that went round and round an interesting track. He would, in all likelihood, have broken the toy in a matter of minutes had he been allowed to touch it, but I did wonder what the point of such a toy was. Infants have to touch things that interest them in order to understand them.

Your child's newfound interest in toys will mean that you can talk to her about them. This will add to her interest in the toys. Eventually it will result in her learning the names for them.

In talking about language development, it is also impossible to ignore the role that perceptual functioning plays in making that development possible. Hearing is crucial, of course. At birth, an infant has been hearing her mother's voice in the womb for about five months. This results in a preference for her mother's voice that has been detected as early as three days after birth—three or four months before she recognizes and prefers her mother's face. Prenatal hearing also results in a general preference for high-pitched voices.

Some infants turn in the direction of unseen sounds at birth. All hearing infants do so by the age of six or seven months. This is known as the localization of sounds, and it is one of the best indications that your child can hear you. Becoming startled by loud, sudden noises is another such indication.

There is some interesting evidence that suggests that infants have a special capacity for perceiving speech sounds. A running vacuum cleaner or a dishwasher is likely to lull a one-month-old infant to sleep. (Really, it is a good trick to use when she is fussy!) But infants of the same age can detect a subtle difference between speech sounds and express interest in this difference.

The ability to see is also important for language development, although less so than the ability to hear. Unfortunately, parents of blind infants may not talk to them as much as parents of sighted infants do because they are not rewarded by their infant's gaze. Most infants can see at birth, though they see poorly. Infants cannot focus as well as adults until four months of age. And not until six months to one year can infants see as acutely as adults.

Much research has examined what infants prefer to look at, and these preferences are good to know if you want to stimulate your child and encourage her to talk to you. Infants can tell one color from another, and they clearly prefer red. Infants also prefer to look at patterns, particularly circular ones. They prefer sharp contrasts to soft, fuzzy ones. In a number of ways, then, the traditional notion of decorating an infant's room in pastels is geared to bore the infant. A room decorated in bright colors and patterns is one that will engage your infant's attention and give her something to coo about.

Much less is known about infants' ability to smell, taste, and feel, compared to how much is known about their ability to see and hear. All that can be said with any confidence is that they can smell, taste, and feel at birth, but they seem to be relatively insensitive in these areas compared to adults.

During the first six months, your child will be working on a number of basic physical skills. She will learn to lift up her head, to roll over, and to sit and stand with some help from you. Perhaps these skills are not as dramatic as walking, but they are indeed remarkable accomplishments. The muscular strength and coordination your child gains from kicking, rolling over, sitting, and standing during her first six months enable her to walk during the next six months just as the practice in vocalizing and the success in communicating during this time enable her to produce fully recognizable language later on.

In all areas of development, then, your child is starting to get organized during her first six months of life. Her major limitation lies in her tendency to forget all about what she does not immediately perceive. Literally, she operates according to the principle of out of sight, out of mind. She will forget you exist the minute you step out of her sight. If she is interested in pawing a delicate Chinese vase, you can easily dissuade her from this by covering the vase with your handkerchief. All the language games in this first section are crucial for your child's development in language, cognition, and emotion.

SINGING 1

Purpose

To calm your crying infant and to give her a sample of language that captures her attention.

Game

Sing frequently to your child. Use such old standards as "Brahms' Lullaby" or make up your own songs. It has been a long time since many new parents sang these songs, so here are the words for a few of the old standards in case you have forgotten them (the tunes are generally more memorable):

Brahms' Lullaby

Lullaby
And good-night.
Go to bed now and sleep tight.
Shut your eyes.
Start to yawn.
Pleasant dreams until the dawn.
When the sun
Lights the sky,
You'll awake
Feeling spry.
Start the day
With a smile.
Life is really worthwhile.

Rock-a-bye Baby

Rock-a-bye baby,
On the tree top.
When the wind blows,
The cradle will rock.
When the bough breaks,
The cradle will fall.
And down will come baby,
Cradle and all.

Twinkle, Twinkle, Little Star

Twinkle, twinkle, little star.
How I wonder what you are.
Up above the world so high,

Like a diamond in the sky.
Twinkle, twinkle, little star.
How I wonder what you are.

Variation

Make up a song or two that uses the baby's name so that she will
get used to hearing it. Every child should have her own song
composed by her parents, even if it is only along the lines of the
following song that I composed for my daughter. (This song works
best if you have a Boston accent and drop your final r's, such as
in the word "weiner." Also, note that "Jessamina" is a nickname
pronounced "Jessameenah.")

Jessamina, mina, mina, mina, mina.
You are a weinah.
Jessamina.
Jessamina, mina, mina, mina, mina.
You are a weinah,
Mina-girl.

Note

Singing is one of the very first *language* games, though it usually
is not thought of that way. Unlike other language games that are
designed to increase vocalizing, this first game usually has the
effect of stopping your child from vocalizing. As I have said, the
human voice, especially a high-pitched one, is one of the best
devices for quieting a crying baby.

Of course, everybody knows that you are supposed to sing to
babies. And everybody knows about "Brahms' Lullaby" and
"Rock-a-bye Baby." But what if you are someone who cannot
carry a tune or who forgets the words or who simply feels awkward singing a full-fledged song? Before my daughter was born,
I could not bring myself to sing in a group of less than two
hundred. So I started out getting used to my rusty voice by simply

humming a few notes in succession. As a matter of fact, some research indicates that babies about two months old prefer to hear rising intonation, so humming a few notes going up the scale worked just as well as "Brahms' Lullaby." Eventually I got into the swing of singing, and now I shamelessly belt out songs to entertain my son even in public places.

One final note on singing: Fetuses can hear at about four months after conception. Parents might try singing one song over and over to their baby in the womb to establish a song that will be familiar and therefore a favorite of the baby's at birth.

OH, YOU BEAUTIFUL BABY

Purpose

To encourage vocalizing and taking turns at vocalizing.

Game

To begin with, your newborn's only vocalization is likely to be crying. But within two months, she will start to coo. This is the time to begin playing what is traditionally the first real language game. Let your baby initiate this game at first. Communicating with your child is like a dance, and since you are quite a bit more skilled in responding appropriately, let your child take the lead. In fact, this is a good first principle throughout much of language development.

Catch your child when she is already cooing. Look her in the eyes, with your face about a foot away from hers so that she can focus on you. Newborns cannot change their focus and can see best at about this distance. When you are in position and have her attention, just smile and begin to talk to her in a high-pitched voice. Abandon your dignity! Chances are, your child will continue to coo in response to your talk and, if you are especially lucky, she will also smile back at you.

Variation

Accompany talk with gestures such as clapping hands or kissing the baby.

Note

Sometimes you can take turns with your child for quite a while. Infants delight in things they seem to be able to control. If you are responding to them, they will get the idea that you are a wonderful toy that they can somehow switch on. Meanwhile, you will be showing them a little bit about how to take turns—a very important part of the communication process.

I usually found myself saying things like "I love you" and "Oh, you bee—yooo—tee-full baby" and "My, you must be feeling happy this morning" to my infant daughter. Really, you can say anything, even "The Dow Jones Industrial Average went up today," since your baby is, of course, far too young to make any sense of what you are saying. But it is important to raise your voice, since most babies respond more to high voices. Women and children have an obvious edge over men in playing this game, but men can achieve success by doing a good falsetto. Although not all children prefer a high-pitched voice, the overwhelming majority do. And I am afraid that many a father, supposedly "enlightened" about the evils of babytalk, has experienced a great deal of frustration in talking to his child, who responds so much to Mom but stops responding as soon as Dad uses his gruff voice.

Many men will resist squeaking at their children at first, but baby smiles are well worth the loss of dignity involved. With a little practice, it will not even seem as though you are doing anything strange, until friends or family unused to being around children overhear you in your new role. A friend of mine was talking to his young daughter one day, when someone overheard them and asked him to lower his voice because he sounded funny. He tried to do so, but as he continued talking to his daughter, it slipped back up again. His daughter became increasingly vocal, and he was not willing or able to violate their special code for very long.

It is important for women, as well as for men, to loosen up and set aside their inhibitions in talking to their children right from the beginning. Varying your tone of voice, using lots of facial expressions, even sticking out your tongue, emphasizing key words such as the child's name—hamming it up, in other words—will maintain your baby's attention much longer than saying things in a more or less flat tone of voice. Accompany this language game with games of patticake and other physical interaction for even more continued attention. Of course, it will be a while until your child plays these games with you, but she will love to watch them even before she can join in. The more you ham it up, the more she will coo.

Although you are more likely to be successful if you let your baby "tell" you when to start playing this game with her, after you both learn it, you can start up rounds with her yourself. The best time to do this is shortly after a nap, when she has just been fed and has had her diaper changed and is generally happy. There are very few things in life more wonderful than a good, long coo song.

WORDS AND DEEDS 1

Purpose

To encourage your child to pay attention to language by watching gestures that are regularly associated with words.

Game

Make up action-word games, such as warning your child that she is about to be tickled ("I'm going to tickle you") or kissed ("Here is the kissing monster") or blown upon ("That old North Wind is blowing and blowing") or raised up high in the air ("*Up* you go and *down* again"). Repeat these routines over and over again each time you play them, and play them often.

Variation

Label some gesture your child makes while she is making it. Pretend that it is a game. For example, if she is waving her arms around, say something like, "Wave to the people. Wave to them. Wave just like Princess Di. Wave to Mommy. Wave to Daddy. Wave to that man over there. Just keep on waving. Wave, wave, wave."

Note

At the age of three months, English-speaking parents traditionally begin to play a series of standard language games that match words with actions: peek-a-boo, patticake, ride-a-cock horse, row, row, row your boat, ring-around-the-rosy. In case you have forgotten these, they go like this:

Say	*Do*
Peek-a-boo	Cover and then uncover your eyes.

*   *   *

Patticake,	Clap baby's hands together.
Patticake,	Clap them together again.
Baker's man.	Clap again.
Bake me a cake	Clap again.
As fast as you can.	Clap again.
Roll it	Make baby's hands roll around each other.
And pound it	Make pounding motion with baby's hands.
And mark it with a *B*.	Draw a *B* with baby's hands.

And put it in the oven	Make motion of putting something in oven.
For baby and me	Kiss your baby.

*   *   *

Ride a cock horse	Hold baby and bounce her on your knee.
To Banbury Cross	Keep bouncing throughout the rhyme.
To see a fine lady	
Upon a white horse.	
Rings on her fingers	Bounce and shake baby's fingers.
And bells on her toes.	Bounce and with one hand tickle toes.
She shall make music	Keep bouncing
Wherever she goes.	

*   *   *

Row, row, row your boat	Take baby's hands and make rowing motion,
Gently down the stream.	Leaning forward while you tip her backward,
Merrilly, merrily,	And vice versa throughout song.
Merrily, merrily.	Life is but a dream.

Be prepared to do most of the work in these games for the next four or five months. Your child will not begin to imitate you until about eight or nine months of age. Long before that, however, she will enjoy anticipating familiar action routines signaled by familiar sounds.

* 2 *

Six to Twelve Months

When your child is about six months old—more a "scooter" than a toddler, really—he will take a major step forward in language development: he will learn how to deliberately open and close his jaw while vocalizing. In short, he will begin to babble. Babbling is the repetition of one syllable, such as "dadadadadada" or "baba-baba" or "mamamamama." Early babbling usually is limited to only a couple of different syllables, somewhat different ones for each child. However, since "mamama" is the easiest sound we can make—just starting up our vocal cords with our mouth in the most relaxed, open position and then occasionally closing it—it is likely to be among the first speech sounds made. "Dadada" is also easy, requiring only minimal tongue control, and also among the first. Actually, a number of studies have found that most infants babble d's before m's, despite the fact that the latter seem easier to adults. So do not be surprised if "dada" emerges before "mama."

These babbled syllables will have no relationship to you or your spouse when your child first utters them, but you now have a clue about an important aspect of language development. Surprisingly enough, parents probably spend more time and effort imitating their children than children do their parents. Mothers of most nations have picked up on the fact that words like "mama" are among the earliest speech sounds practiced by their children and have decided to reward themselves for their child-raising efforts by making "mama" the official name that all young children are supposed to call their mother.

Over the next few months, several important things happen. First, your child's babbling will progress from repetitions of a few easily produced syllables to a rich mirror of many of the speech sounds of your mutual native language. American mothers can tell an American baby's babbling from that of a Russian or Chinese baby's. Such babbling is the cutting edge of genuine communication. A one-year-old child will act as if he is talking (and seem very proud of it) and yet make almost no sense much of the time even to his own parents.

Second, somewhere between eight and ten months, your child will begin to imitate you, and this opens up the chance to play a number of language games in this section.

Third, some of your child's babbling will become hooked up to people and objects to form his first "words." Some of your child's first words will be pronounced with astonishing clarity. Others are words only you really can understand. You will know that "baba" means that your ten-month-old wants his bottle, "caa" means that the cat has come into the room, "gaa" means that something really interesting is going on, and so forth. But your neighbor may not be able to appreciate your child's accomplishments.

Your child will not only invent pronunciations, he may also invent words for things. You will eventually realize that "uggles" means "popsicles." Enjoy these invented words. Acknowledge that you understand him and provide the correct word: "Uggles? Oh you want a popsicle. I see." Or say, "Yes, that's right. That is an elephant," even if the child has said something like "efflunt." Sometimes even you may be unable to understand what your child is trying to say. He may become very impatient with your dull-wittedness. Keep trying.

At this point, do not worry about pronunciation. Children take until elementary school to sort out all the fine points of pronunciation. Accept the version of a word that your child produces. *Accepting what he says while still providing the proper pronunciation are the key ingredients of successful language acquisition.* And a child's pronunciation of words, though incorrect, is something to be treasured. It is another of those signs that your child is not a tape recorder but is instead inventing the language for himself. Related to this is the fact that these first efforts are going to be your child's original inventions. I so enjoy this aspect of language development that I keep track of many of the inventions I come across in children I meet. Some of my favorites appear in this book. You may want to make a note of your own child's inventions.

Actually, children often will recognize the correct pronunciation of a word some time before they can produce the correct form themselves. Many people have anecdotes like the following about children with temporary lisps, for example. The child points to his dog and says, "Lathy."

His uncle replies, "Lathy?"

"No. Lathy."

"Oh, you mean *Lassie.*"

The child nods. "Lathy."

Eventually most children can and do correct their own pronunciation. You do not have to give them specific instruction in it. In fact, you may put them off if you do.

Generally, children have at least one word by ten months and several by twelve months. These words will typically mean something like the adult versions but will not be identical to them. For example, your child may say "caa" every time the family pet or his stuffed cat or a picture of a cat comes into view, but he also will say "caa" to pictures of birds and pigs and dogs and in greeting a grandparent.

Another of the most important linguistic accomplishments during this time occurs silently and is actually, oddly, the loss of an ability. Janet Werker and her colleagues have discovered that while infants aged six to eight months can discriminate speech sounds even of languages to which they are not exposed, some time between the ages of ten and twelve months they lose this ability. Babies who hear foreign languages during this time, however, will retain the ability to discern the speech sounds used in those languages even into adulthood. Parents who expose their children to foreign languages during this particular age will facilitate their children's ability to understand those languages later on even if the parents do not themselves speak those languages at home.

It is very important to realize that there are large individual differences during this period of development. Most children babble, some quite a bit, others less so. Some children reportedly never babble, yet they still develop normal language.

There are also considerable differences in children's willingness to imitate their parents on cue. Some children are virtual parrots. They imitate almost anything they hear. I know one child who had an impressive number of physical routines he would perform for an audience at the slightest encouragement (for example, he would hold up his finger to his parents' cry of "Joey's number one"; he would spread his hands wide to "Joey's sooooo big"; he would do all the appropriate gestures to "patticake"). His language soon reflected this tendency to imitate. He would repeat whole segments of his parents' refrains to him, although it was clear that he did not really understand the individual words.

Other children are not so imitative. Instead, they are more analytic or reflective. They listen to things that are said to them, think about them for a while, and come up with words when they are ready. I do not think my daughter ever played a game of patticake in her life that I did not drag her hands through. She just stared at me when I tried to get her to do it more or less on her own. Children who do not imitate readily will learn language just as well as children who do. But parents of nonimitative children may not have much success with imitation games.

Whereas babbling, a major milestone in language development, usually begins at six months, new milestones in emotional, cognitive, and physical development usually happen a month or so later and are very interrelated. At about seven months you will notice that your baby often cries when you leave the room. Up to this point, he has been relatively easy to leave with babysitters because he forgets about you when you are not around. But between seven and eight months of age, he develops the ability to remember that you exist even if you are not around. Now, frequently, when you leave the room, you will trigger a howl of protest from him. When you return, you may be greeted at first with smiles, then later with words and smiles, as his language develops, though sometimes your departure will upset him more than usual and he may need some extra hugging. Attachment theorists refer to this as the development of person permanence.

Often the onset of person permanence coincides with the development of a fear of strangers, though sometimes the fear occurs later. Your baby who used to smile at completely unknown people in line at the grocery store will now resist going to your best friend, who has seen him before but not often enough to warrant his trust. Some babies become very afraid of strangers at this time, others show less fear. How much fear of strangers any particular child will show depends upon his attachment to his parent, his temperament, and his experience with strangers.

The second major aspect of emotional development occurs when your baby begins to crawl during this age range. It is at this point that he is capable of seeking you out. He knows you still exist even when he cannot see you. He does not like to be out of sight of you. He now has the means of correcting what to him is a bad situation. So he crawls around looking for you. Or he follows you out of rooms.

Babies from seven months to about three years are clingy, cuddly little creatures. This is a normal, desirable sign of healthy attachment. This is the phase of emotional development known as the phase of active initiative in seeking proximity and contact. The name explains the phase very well. All your interaction with your young infant culminates in his full-blown attachment to you at this time.

The major cognitive development during this time is the development of object permanence. Previously, if your child was interested in playing with something he should not have been playing with, all you had to do was cover it up. He would forget about it once it was out of his sight. But at eight months, this will change. He will develop the ability to remember objects even when he is not directly perceiving them. Games such as peek-a-boo and toys such as jack-in-the-box play with the appearance and disappearance of interesting objects. They capitalize on this new-found memory of ability and are big hits at this time.

With his development of object permanence, your infant becomes capable of setting his own goals. I have already mentioned one of the major goals he will set continually, namely, the goal of being close to you. But there are other goals that are not nearly so delightful. For example, for some reason, most babies must have some built-in electrical outlet detector. Your child will find electrical outlets you never knew you had sometime around his first birthday. You need to be prepared to interrupt his determination to explore these intriguing holes in the wall. One of the least effective ways of doing this is to spank him after he has. had a chance to fondle the outlet. Both the spanking and the timing are ineffective. One of the best ways to stop his interest in outlets before it really blossoms is to yell "NO," clap your hands loudly, and bang something loud enough to startle him as he is reaching for the outlet. This will have the short-term effect of making him cry and, after several repetitions, the long-term effect of making him a little phobic about outlets, which is just what you want.

Research indicates that babies are not born with full adult depth perception. It is an ability that must develop after birth and probably after experience moving around the world. When he is about eight months old, your infant will develop the ability to perceive depths. You will realize this because he will become afraid of sudden drop-offs. Unfortunately, this is an ability that emerges gradually. In the process of learning about depths, your baby probably will fall or take a few headers off beds (one hopes not from any greater height, although it does happen).

It's impossible to discuss development in other areas without mentioning physical development. During this time, your baby will learn to sit and stand on his own. He will learn to crawl on his belly at about eight months and to creep around on hands and knees at about ten or eleven months. And finally, he will learn to walk at about twelve months.

Looking at individual babies, it seems as if they shuttle their attention between work on their physical abilities and work on their language skills at this time. For example, my son first babbled at five and a half months, but quit doing so after a few days. He resumed babbling at seven and a half months—after he had mastered the art of sitting, which he had been unable to do prior to his vacation from babbling. In general, a number of babies babble quite reliably and with increasing complexity during this time.

With all of these impressive accomplishments, it is easy to lose sight of the limitations your child has at this time. He still is thinking in a very sensorimotor sort of way. He needs to touch you and see you to feel safe. He does not have the cognitive or language ability to understand your plans. If he wants to be hugged, he needs to be hugged right then. He cannot understand your need to finish stirring the soup or writing a letter before you hug him. He also cannot understand where you are going when you leave, nor can he understand that you will be coming back in a few hours. All the things required to reach that understanding will be beyond him until after he turns three years old. For that reason, lengthy separations of a week or more when your child is seven months to three years should be avoided if at all possible.

Toddler Talk, Words and Deeds 2, Can You Say, and Book Reading 1 are all important games to play at this time because they are crucial for developing language. The rest of the games in this section are for fun.

TODDLER TALK

Purpose

To express affection and to provide your child with language that is simplified enough for him to acquire.

Game

Babbling indicates that your child has become much more interested in language; many parents find themselves taking this into
account by speaking a special form of language that I have dubbed
"toddler talk" in order to avoid the stigma that has been attached
to "babytalk." It is a very good idea to speak toddler talk to your
child since children prefer to listen to it and consequently pay
more attention to it than to adult talk.

Toddler talk is language that is simplified to help your child
learn language. It is primarily an adult's way of expressing affection while presenting language that children have a good chance
of understanding. Here are the general guidelines for this language game, but remember that your child's attention is what you
are after, and children do differ.

1. Use a high voice until your child is four or five years old.
2. Change your tone of voice a lot, exaggerate words, even
whisper at times. Whispering works especially well to get the
attention of two-year-olds.
3. Simplify your sentences.
4. Shorten your sentences.
5. Slow down your rate of speaking.
6. Speak distinctly, especially when your child is fifteen to
sixteen months old and is beginning to use words regularly.
7. Talk to your child a lot, even if he is not yet talking back.
It may seem silly to you to do this, but there is evidence that
hearing a lot of language will help your child to learn language.
The more you talk, the more he will, too.
8. At six months, talk about concrete things, things you point
out to your child while you are talking to him. Better yet, talk
about things he is looking at already. Children do not have much
ability to think about things that are not there in front of them until
the age of a year and a half to two years. You may notice that this
is a shift from what you probably talked about when your child
was an infant, namely, his feelings. This shift reflects the fact that

your child has become increasingly interested in the world around him.

9. Draw attention to the endings of words by saying things like "dogg-y," "dadd-y," "kitt-y," and so forth. Or make long pauses after words. Or kiss your baby on his nose at the end of each word. Or use lots of rhymes—make them up as you go along or recite standard nursery rhymes and songs.

A lot of parents, myself included, find themselves a bit rusty in recalling nursery rhymes. My solution was to make up rhymes myself. For example, when I was trying to feed my nine-month-old son, Nick, I sang:

> Open up, open up, open up.
> Open up, Buttercup.

He usually got enough of a charge out of this rhyme to open his mouth for another bite.

When he pulled himself up in his crib, he was treated to:

> He's standing tall.
> He's not so small.
> I hope he won't fall.
> He's standing tall.

This became one of his three-year-old sister's favorites, and she chanted it to him as well.

When Nick was in the Johnny Jump-Up, he got his own rap song, of sorts:

> He's a fine bouncing baby boy.
> He's our pride.
> He's our joy.
> He's kind of coy.
> He has a ploy
> For making noise,

> He plays with toys.
> He won't annoy.
> He's a fine bouncing baby boy.

At various times during the day, Nick was treated to a rhyme based on my daughter's nickname for him, which was "Nickle."

> Give me a Nickle
> And I'll buy a pickle.
> A pickle for a Nickle today.
> Give me a Nickle,
> And I'll give him a tickle.
> A tickle for a Nickle today.

High art it's not, but Nick enjoyed these rhymes.

Remember that your child can use some help in figuring out what a word is. We adults hear a sentence as a series of words with definite beginnings and endings, but in fact a spoken sentence is usually a continuous stream of sound. Think of what it is like to hear a sentence in a foreign language if you do not believe this. What are the words there?

10. As your child grows older and begins to pick up words, stress all the syllables in words he shows interest in repeating. If you do not stress all the syllables, chances are that he will not hear the unstressed ones and you will leave them out.

11. Repeat what your child says and what you yourself say. Mothers of very verbal children repeat their children's utterances and otherwise relate what they say to what their children say. They do not simply lecture their children.

12. When you talk to your child, make sure that most of the time he is attentive. Call his name, hug or kiss him, manipulate interesting objects (squeak ducks, shake rattles, play with puppets, and so forth). Do anything to get his attention. Since babies get bored with things very quickly, you will have to do a variety of things to maintain his attention. However, if you try several times to get his attention and he persists in looking at his toes rather than

at you, do not force the issue. Play the game with him another time. He is probably sleepy.

13. Always give your child a chance to respond to what you say. Simply providing an unbroken stream of speech will drown his interest. But waiting for him to respond with a gurgle or in whatever way he chooses will ensure his continued attention. Some research indicates that his responding may be at least as beneficial as hearing you talk.

14. Concentrate on making statements about things and asking your child questions. Some parents speak to their children much as a drill sergeant does, continually commanding them to do something. While all parents need to speak this way at times, the bulk of your speech to your child should not be orders. Because it is especially easy to become a drill sergeant when you are tired or upset, it is important to be on guard against this tendency—it will usually only make matters worse for you by upsetting your child and precipitating a temper tantrum.

15. Above all, enjoy yourself and use this special way of talking to express your affection for your child. When you listen to parents speaking to their children in this special way, it is hard to tell what is language instruction and what is affection. After all, expressing affection is the best reason for playing this game.

Note

Some very good studies indicate that the more a child hears toddlers talk (researchers call it "child-directed speech"), the more rapidly he will acquire language and the higher his IQ will be. Other studies show us how important this sort of talk is by looking at children who have not heard it. Some deaf parents with hearing children have tried to get their children to learn language by having them listen to television. This strategy does not work. Such children do not acquire language until adults talk to them directly, making the sorts of modifications I have mentioned here.

We are indebted to Catherine Snow, Jean Berko Gleason, and others for articulating the rules of this game. Their work is among the most interesting research going on today in child development. In fact, many psychologists feel that these researchers are developing the most promising theory of language development since Chomsky's (see pp. 10–12).

If you remain unconvinced that you should play this game, you can try an experiment yourself. Say something to your child in the voice you use to talk to your adult friends. Then say the same thing in toddler talk, and see which one makes your child smile and respond more. Do not think of it as "talking down" but rather as "talking *to*" your child.

WORDS AND DEEDS 2

Purpose

To encourage your child to pay attention to language by making standard gestures that are associated with standard words.

Games

Play standard language games that match words with actions: peek-a-boo, patticake, ride-a-cock horse, row, row, row your boat, ring-around-the-rosy. Your child is now old enough to do some of the gestures himself. (See Words and Deeds 1 for these old favorites.)

Variations

1. Begin to encourage your child to imitate waving goodbye while saying "Bye-Bye" or "Hi."
2. Invent your own games associating language with gestures. For example, say, "Jake's number one" and hold up your index finger on "one." Or say, "Alex is soooo big," and stretch your arms apart.

3. Encourage your child to do games all by himself, showing off his routines for family and friends.

RHYTHMS

Purpose

To encourage rough vocal imitation and attention to the rhythms of language.

Game

Repeat any nonsense syllable of your choice ("bup" or "glub" or "boomp" are good ones) two or three times, wait for your child to respond, and reward him by laughing or hugging him when he has repeated any (even unrelated) sound the same number of times. Interrupt him when he reaches the right number, if necessary, to keep him from going beyond it. For example, say, "glup, glup, glup." Wait. He says, "lub, lub, lub," when you interrupt and say, "Great!"

Variation

When your child has mastered matching the number of sounds you say, switch to stressing different syllables. For example, say, "Blum *dab* dum, blum *dab* dum." Reward your child no matter what he says, but be especially encouraging if he matches your stress patterns.

ANIMAL NOISES

Purpose

To encourage vocal imitation.

Game

Make any noise that is similar to a noise your child has just made. For example, if he has just babbled, "mmmm," you say "moo." If he repeats the sound, laugh and hug him.

Variations

1. Page through a picture book of animals and imitate the sounds that each animal makes. Older children will begin to produce the sounds associated with various animals.

2. Machine noises are not nearly as widely appreciated as animal noises are, although machines make a number of sounds and actions that your child will notice. Of course, most children learn that trains go choo-choo and clocks go tick-tock, or at least old-fashioned ones do. But get your child to say that cars go "whoosh," fans go "round and round," elevators go "up and down," planes go "neeeowwwwwww," boats go "putputputput," blenders go "blaaatt," and so forth. Just make sure that you use the same version of the sound every time you play the game.

SINGING 2

Purpose

To encourage physical and vocal imitation.

Game

Sing a few songs repeatedly, and reward your child for any imitation he comes up with. At first children will imitate the tune by humming. As they grow older, they will begin to imitate at least some of the words.

Variation

Make up a song that uses gestures and words about your child, such as, "Jess (point to child) is so tall (stretch your arms to show height of child), tall as a wall (point to wall). Jess (point to child) is so sweet, sweet as a treat (point to candy or cake). Jess is so cute, cute as a flute (make gesture of playing pretend flute). Jess is so happy (grin broadly), happy as a puppy (point to puppy or toy dog). Jess is so sad (make sad face), sad as a tadpole (make swimming motions for tadpole or picture of tadpole). Jess is so nice, nice as mice (squeal and make gesture of tail of mouse or mouse eating)." And so forth. Sing the words to whatever tune comes to mind or chant them.

CAN YOU SAY?

Purpose

To encourage your child to imitate your speech sounds.

Game

Mr. Rogers gets far too much credit for playing this language game. Actually, many parents begin to play this game just as soon as their child begins to babble at about six months, although they are not likely to have much success until the child is at least eight months old. There are only a couple of rules for playing the game. First, try to get your child to imitate a word that sounds similar to the sound he has just babbled. Second, try to make the word the name of some object or person he is looking at. For example, if your child has just said, "dadadada" and his father is nearby, say "Can you say 'Dada'?" If his father is not present, but a toy duck is, say "Can you say 'duck'?" Hug, shake, or otherwise manipulate the object that the word refers to as you say it just to call attention to it. But the main point of this game is to get the child to imitate language sounds, so do not worry too much about hooking up the word with what it meant. That will come later.

Variation

When your child is used to playing the game, you can introduce new speech sounds (ones that he has not yet babbled) and try to get him to imitate these.

Note

Some children are more inclined to imitate parents on command than are other children. Children who do not imitate on command as much seem quite able to copy sounds—they may even wind up having larger vocabularies than more imitative children—but they will produce a word some time after they have heard it. In other words, they will imitate a word when they want to communicate with it. So do not be upset if it takes a while for your child to imitate you or if he never seems to play this game. I suspect many parents suffer a lot of frustration as rounds of "Can you say" are ignored time after time.

Eventually, at least some of the time, your child will respond in some way. If he comes back with anything at all like the word you were trying to get him to imitate, say, "Dada?" or "Duck? Good boy!" Remember that the most important goal of any language game is communication. Whenever you are instructing your child in pronunciation or grammar, the best way to do it is to provide the opportunity for self-correction by repeating whatever he is trying to say rather than saying something like, "No, that's wrong. You say '*duck*' not 'duh,'" which would make you sound crabby, not like a parent who is really interested in what his child is trying to say. Simply repeating what your child is trying to say in correct form will let the child know you are listening to him and give him a model sentence to use when he is ready to do so.

BOOK READING

Purpose

To encourage an interest in books.

Props

Any of the Golden Touch and Feel Books, such as *The Touch Me Book* or *Pat the Bunny.*

Game

Show your child how to touch things in the book and turn the pages. Name a few things, but do not bother trying to read what is written since your young child will want to perform the various touches and turn pages fast. Name the same things in more or less the same way every time you read the book.

Variation

Let your child page through (even destroy) old magazines. Talk to him about pictures that interest him.

Note

Some research indicates that the single largest factor in a child's later achievement in school is the amount of time that he is read to at home. Reading books with your child should be a daily event that begins now.

✳ 3 ✳

Twelve to Eighteen Months

At thirteen months, your child probably will understand fifty words, though she can produce only a half dozen or so. Therefore, at this age, your child will be working very hard learning words for things. She will progress from imitating speech sounds more or less randomly to using regular sounds to refer to objects, and a number of games in this section are designed to facilitate this process.

Not only will your child be working very hard to learn vocabulary, but you will be working very hard to teach her vocabulary, whether you realize it or not. You will find yourself repeating a few words over and over again. Your child will reward you eventually by producing the words herself. However, she may produce a word one day and seemingly forget it the next. Such lapses are quite normal.

Your child will be unlikely to learn the words she hears most frequently, which are "a," "an," and "the." Nor will she name the objects she has seen most frequently, for example, the ceiling, wall, or floor. Instead, in the beginning stages of language learning, she probably will name objects that change, especially objects that she herself can change or manipulate. Over half of the first fifty words your child learns are likely to be general names for things, such as "bow-wow" for dog, "ba" for ball, "cow," and "button."

Your child probably will begin asking "Whatdat" and pointing out things for you to name. Children seem programmed to learn language. Talking to your child is necessary for her language development, but it is nice to know that she comes highly equipped for accomplishing such a complex task.

When she speaks at this age, your child will say one word at a time, although what is one word to her may be more to us as with "Whatdat." She never says "what" or "dat" by themselves, so it counts as one word from her perspective.

At this age your child will scatter her early words throughout her babble, which has become so wordlike that you could mistake it for a foreign language. Perhaps it would be more accurate to say that you can decipher only part of her babble as legitimate words. She may intend to say more words, which fall on deaf ears.

Keep talking to your child as she babbles away, along with playing all the other language games you have played so far. Use basic names for things during this stage when you talk to your child. For example, use "chair" rather than "furniture" or "rocking chair." Such basic names are easier for your child to pick up. As she becomes more familiar with chairs, then you can begin to use more specific words. Also be consistent, as I point out elsewhere. Do not call something a "chair" one day and a "stool" the next.

By eighteen months, your child will have a vocabulary of up to fifty words. She may begin combining two of these at a time, as in "ba(d) ca(t)." Of course it is important to realize that there are large individual differences in language ability at this age, and that these early individual differences are rather meaningless.

In fact, such early differences probably have more to do with what parents have been doing with their children than with the children's capacity. One researcher found that the single most important predictor of intelligence scores at the age of three is how much time a child is talked to by adults. Television and overheard adult conversation do not count. Playing language games is crucial for developing your child's ability to think.

Many (but not all) parents find that during this time, their children begin to talk to themselves in their cribs prior to falling asleep at night. Psychologists have studied such crib speech and find that it contains much valuable language practice. Children will continue to engage in crib speech until they are three years old.

One word of warning: some children do not talk much or connect two words at a time until they are two and a half years old. If your child is not talking by eighteen months, your pediatrician no doubt will tell you not to worry. However, I question this advice. If you have been talking to your child a lot, playing all the games discussed so far, and your child still does not respond by this age, you should consider having her hearing checked. Roughly one-third of all children with seriously impaired hearing are not diagnosed as such until the age of three, when they still have little or no language. The problem with waiting until three years for diagnosis is that those years are very important for language acquisition. If a hearing test reveals no impairment, continue to play language games with your child or even increase how much time you spend doing this. It may be frustrating for you, but hide these feelings.

Now that your child is a toddler, it is very easy to observe how she uses you as what Mary Ainsworth calls a secure base. When you are in a strange room with your child, the world is very interesting to her. She will toddle over and play with some toys or visit with her grandmother. She will smile, laugh, and vocalize. The minute you step out of the unfamiliar room, however, things change dramatically. Your child usually cries, protesting your departure. The once attractive toys are of no interest whatsoever to your child when you are gone. In fact, attempts by strangers to distract her by playing with the toys often meet with dismal failure. Sometimes even Grandma, whom she knows and usually enjoys, can turn into a scary person whose hugs are met with resistance and further screaming instead of reciprocation.

Working parents may find that they have to face a heart-wrenching protest every morning when they leave for work. Remind yourself in this situation that this protest is a sign of your child's attachment to you. Some children never seem to get used to parents leaving during this age span. A good caretaker will be able to calm your child down and get her to play after you leave, however. Moreover, your child will outgrow such strong protests, especially if you are emotionally available to her when at home. That is, if you pay your child a lot of attention in the evenings and on weekends, there is good evidence that such daily departures need not affect the quality of your relationship.

When you return, all is right with the world again. Your child will greet you and usually demand to be picked up. Pick the child up. Again, you need to postpone your needs at this stage of the child's life. Such young children may read repeated postponement of affection as rejection. Not until three can they begin to really understand your plans and needs.

A child's first birthday marks a difficult transition for parents. For twelve months you have been doing everything you possibly could to stop your child from crying. Now that she can walk, she can get into a lot more trouble than she could before. In other words, you need to begin to discipline her. This calls for some serious thoughts on your part. It is very difficult to encapsulate all that developmental psychology has to say about discipline. Generally speaking, it is a good idea to set a few rules and stick by them. Explain the reasons for those rules, but remember you are speaking to a young child whose language is very limited. Explain the reason for rules by demonstrating or acting out. For example, show her that if she pushes the cup off the table it will spill and make a big mess by spilling a little of the contents and labeling it "mess." Early on, take the opportunity when she accidentally hurts herself to say "Hurt, you hurt yourself." Make a big deal of what "hurt" means. Repeat it whenever appropriate. Then you can use that term when you tell her not to cross the street alone or not to walk down steps by herself.

A number of rules that you will find yourself setting are prohibitions that have to do with the effect of your child's behavior on you. For example, the real reason you want her to stop making a loud noise (when no one but you is around) is that it hurts your ears. Now is the time to get into some good habits yourself concerning the language of discipline. Don't say, "You bad girl!" when what you really mean is, "Stop that. I don't like it because it hurts my ears." Talk about the effect an action has on you. Tell your child why you don't like something.

The language of discipline will become a habit for you. "Bad girl" and "bad boy" are shorthand ways of saying that you do not care for something the child is doing. It may seem to you that "bad girl" and "Stop pinching me, you are hurting my arm" mean the same thing, especially to a young child. But while your child may not grasp the distinction now, she soon will. "Bad girl" is a generalizable expression that can be built into the child's self-concept with enough repetitions, becoming perhaps a self-fulfilling prophecy, perhaps a contribution to chronic depression, or both. "Stop pinching me, you are hurting my arm" is a specific request and an explanation of your request. It may seem as though your child should know that she is hurting you. It may seem too obvious to mention, but that is not the case.

From twelve to eighteen months, your child will be in what Piaget calls the stage of elaboration of objects. She will delight in doing a variety of different things with some object. Often you will observe this while feeding her. At first she will eat the oatmeal, for example. Then she will begin to put her fingers in it. Perhaps she will begin to smear it around the tray table of her high chair. After she tires of that, she may take to wiping the oatmeal in her hair and then to dropping great gobs of it over the side and watching it fall. Your first reaction may be that she is making a huge mess, and of course that is true. But Piaget's great insight into this common event in the lives of babies is that your child is thinking about the object. Again, she thinks by manipulating. Her advance over previous stages is the variety of things she thinks of to do with the oatmeal, more than you yourself might have imagined possible. Keep this insight in mind at such times when you discover the aftermath of her "thoughts." You will probably tell your child that you do not enjoy her activities with the oatmeal. You also should realize that this is why Playdough was invented.

At this age, your child can find things she has seen disappear. She cannot find things she has not seen disappear. Hide-and-seek will not be a successful game at this time, unless you modify it to take into account your child's limitations. Call her attention to yourself as you disappear behind a tree, and encourage her to run after you. But do not move to another hiding place out of her sight. That would be a nasty trick, since she will not know what to do to find you and quite likely will become disconsolate.

Your child's perceptual abilities were pretty much in place at the end of the last section. She can see, hear, taste, smell, and feel very much what you do. Physically, she literally is going to make great strides during this time. She will learn to walk backward and up steps. She may learn to kick and throw a ball. She will start to scribble spontaneously, so crayons are a must at this time.

The more your child can do, the more ways there are to have fun with her. A number of games in the following section are just for fun. But the games that are particularly important in language development are Words and Things 1, Test Questions, Expansions, and At Least One Book Every Day.

WORDS AND THINGS 1

Purpose

To encourage your child to hook up sounds to things, to help her vocalizations to start to mean something.

Game

Once your child is successfully imitating sounds that you make, you can shift your attention to hooking up sounds to things. That is, you can begin to work on your child's vocabulary. At first, you will probably want to focus on only a few names, most likely "Mama," "Dada," "Puppup," and "Kitty." Name something and then talk about it while you draw attention to it in some way. For example, you might say "*Kitty*, there's a good *kitty*. Can you pet the *kitty*?" First words require patience and many repetitions by parents.

It's a very good idea to name more than one example of something at a time. Point to all the bears or bunnies or lights or hot things around you and call them by the same name: "This is a bunny, and that is a bunny, and that is a bunny and this is a bunny." In this way, your child will be able to figure out what all bunnies, for example, have in common. Point out the distinctive features of things: "See the long ears and the fluffy white tail?"

Variations

1. Name things that your child points out. She increasingly will point out things and request their names, probably accompanying her point with a grunt of "whatdat" or "mmmphh." She even may decide to point to a dozen different things in a row, which some adults find annoying but which really can be seen as an amusing game.

2. One particular version of this game proves to be especially fun. I call it "Mama's eyes, Baby's eyes." Point to all the features of a face (and later body) that you and your child share: "Mama's eyes, Billy's eyes, Mama's nose, Billy's nose, Mama's mouth, Billy's mouth, Mama's chin, Billy's chin," etc.

Note

There is some evidence that the more you say "That is a _____," the sooner your child will master things like plural endings for nouns. So point out a lot of examples of things and name them, always beginning with, "This is a _____," or "That is an _____," or "Those are _____."

Talking more about the things you name may help your child to develop a larger vocabulary of general names. So do not stop when pointing something out and giving it a name. Tell your child what it does while you show her what you are talking about. Consider the following dialogue: Adult: "This is a *truck*. It's a *yellow truck* like this sweater. Trucks are *big*. You can make it go like this. There are some more *trucks* over there." Child: "Tuck." Adult: "That's right. Truck." When you play this language game, you are teaching your child the words "truck" and "yellow," the plural ending *s*, and something about the nature of trucks—that they go in a certain way and are big. In addition to all that, you will maintain your child's interest in the whole exercise by manipulating the toy in an interesting way.

Even though you talk a lot about the things you name, be sure to emphasize consistent labels for things. Do not call something a lamp one day, a light the next, and a goose (lamp) the next. Decide on the names you will use to begin with and stick to these. As a rule, it is better to tackle the most general names for things to begin with: "bear," "light," "girl," "truck" are more useful for starters than "Pooh bear," "floor lamp," "Marcia," or "dump truck."

Almost all parents engage in some form of this game. But many parents are not so much interested that their children acquire language as they are that their children obey the parents' orders and master language enough to do this. Consequently, the language game of vocabulary building is often played more like in the following monologue: "Drop that fork. Don't play with that *fork*. I said to put down that fork." The child eventually will learn the word "fork," but it is hardly as pleasant an interchange as the previous one. The use of language is an exchange of emotions as well as of information.

TEST QUESTIONS

Purpose

To test your child's comprehension of certain words, to encourage her production of a word, and to get her used to naming things.

Game

When your child understands words for things, ask her, "Where is the cat?" or "Where is your nose?" When your child can produce words for things, ask, "What is that?" while pointing to the picture of something you know she knows the word for. If your child does not respond or responds incorrectly, avoid saying that she is wrong. Instead, simply give the right answer: "Oh, I thought that was the cat."

Note that this game is especially successful if played while reading a book.

Variations

1. During dinner, ask your child where a particular food is or what that (dessert) is, and give her the food when she points out or names it correctly.

2. When you buy your child a set of animals or a puzzle with different (whole) things in it, give her the things as she names them.

3. Switch roles. You name things that your child knows the name of. Deliberately make mistakes and encourage your child to correct you.

EXPANSIONS

Purpose

To let your child know you have heard her, to check to make sure that you have understood her correctly, to show her that conversation is a series of related comments, and to provide a model of a more correct way of saying something that is not too complicated for her to understand.

Game

When your child says something, respond by recasting what she has just said in correct but simple language. For example, your child says, "ba" and you say, "Yes, that is a *bottle*." Or your child says, "ba ca" and you say, "Yes, he is a *bad cat*." Or your child says, "mmmm" and you say, "Yes, cows say *moo*."

Variation

Combine this with the Can You Say? game, alternating saying something for your child to imitate with expanding what she says by way of imitation and you have a toddler conversation. It might go something like this: You say, "Can you say doggie? That is a doggie. Say doggie." Your child says, "Og." You say, "Yes, the doggie is barking."

Note

Some research shows that continually expanding your child's statements is associated with advanced language development. Researchers speculate that the reason expansion helps your child to learn language is that they allow the child to shift her attention from the content of what you are saying (she knows this because she said it herself) to the form, which is a more correct one than she provided.

CLOCKS GO _____

Purpose

To engage your child in rather formal turn-taking, to teach her action words, to encourage her to form sentences, and to introduce her to sets of sentences.

Props

No props are needed, but you need to point to the real action described when teaching your child a new action term.

Game

When your child knows at least a half dozen animal noises and other action words, name some objects and ask her to name their actions in sequence (her answers are in italics): Wheels go *round and round*, clocks go *tick-tock*, trains go *choo-choo*, seesaws go *up and down*, cats go *meow*, etc. Add a new action word each time you play the game.

Variation

As your child becomes accustomed to this routine and as she approaches eighteen months, begin to play the game as always and then point to something like a cat and encourage her to say the whole sentence. "Ca' yow" is a major accomplishment for an eighteen-month-old child.

Note

Parents are likely to play this game with animal noises, especially since there are so many first books that are of this sort, but they may not take full advantage of the structure that is established in the process. Children at this age know a number of action words, and any action word they know can be requested in this sequence. I found this game useful when my child was rebelling against having her diaper changed or was making a scene in a restaurant. Sometimes your child simply will not be interested in listening to you no matter how well you sing or talk, but she will show an interest in doing the talking herself. Crying is not as much fun as talking when you have something to talk about.

HER OWN STORY

Purpose

To get your child used to hearing storytelling language.

Game

When your child is able to produce a few words and to understand a few more, you can get her used to listening to a story by
making one up that uses her vocabulary. Be sure to keep the story
short and to really emphasize the words she understands by repeating them and stressing them. The story does not have to make
a lot of sense. Just using many of the words she knows at one time
will delight her. It might go something like this, with the italicized
words being those your child knows and the ones that you stress:

> Once upon a time, there was a *cat*. The *cat* was a *bad cat*,
> a very *bad cat*. And he went for a walk in the woods, where
> he met a *cow*. The *cat* said *hi* to the *cow*. The *cow* said *moo* to
> the *cat*. Then the *cat* stole a *button* from the cow's shirt. The
> *bad cat* said *bye-bye* to the *cow* and he went home. And they
> all lived happily ever after. Except the *cow* who says *moo* lost
> her *button*. What a *bad cat* that was.

Of course, as your child acquires a larger vocabulary, you can
invent a number of different stories. Be sure to repeat them, so she
will be able to remember them.

Variations

1. If your child has certain routines that she does with you,
include them in your story and let her say them. For example, if
your child always says "moo" when you say, "Cows go _____,"
then be sure to let her do that to keep her attention engaged in the
story.

2. If your child develops a favorite among the stories you

make up for her in her own words, you may want to write down some version of it and either draw pictures or collect pictures to go along with the words. In the preceding story, for example, you might draw a picture of a bad cat taking a walk, a cow dressed in a shirt and standing in some woods, the cat waving to the cow, the cow mooing, the cat stealing a button from the cow's shirt, the cat waving good-bye to the cow, and the cow looking forlornly down at her missing button. Accompany each picture with the appropriate printed words.

3. Some parents really expand this game. They make up a story for their child every night for years, eventually settling on a particular character or set of characters. My husband makes up a story for my daughter about a little animal named Bucky every night, and has done so for a couple of years. Often the little animal has adventures and worries similar to those of my daughter, giving her a chance to talk about these things with her father. At three and a half, my daughter began suggesting to her father what "The Worry" was going be for the evening story.

AT LEAST ONE BOOK EVERY DAY

Purpose

To introduce your child to the sounds of written language and to the link between sounds and graphic symbols.

Props

Where's Spot? (Putnam), *Good Night Moon* (Harper Collins), or any other simple book.

Game

Page through books and name and comment on pictures that your child points to, as you have been doing, but this time read at least some of the printed words while you point to the object and word you are pronouncing. Say standard things like "Bears go grrr" repeatedly. It is better to play this game with a few books repeatedly than with a lot of books only a few times. If, while reading, you lose your child's attention, shift to telling the story in your own words. Act it out. Ham it up.

Variation

Leave out words that your child anticipates after many repetitions and that you know she can produce. For example, looking at a picture of a cow that is accompanied by the words, "Cows say moo," leave out the "moo" and look at her until she says it.

Note

A researcher named G.J. Whitehurst and his colleagues did a remarkably simple and effective experiment with book-reading. They had some parents of 21- to 36-month-old children read books at home for a month just as they usually did. The researchers instructed other parents to talk more with their young children about what they were reading. Specifically, such parents were told to ask more questions of their children and to do straight reading less than they used to do. Parents were encouraged to ask children to talk about what was read: "What do you think that cat is feeling here?" or "What is that truck doing over there?" Parents in the special group also were encouraged to repeat or expand upon anything their children voluntarily said about the story. (See also Test Questions and Expansions. These parents were discouraged from administering directives to "be quiet" or "turn the page" as well as from asking questions that could be answered by having the child simply point to something on the page. After only one month of such a simple program, children in the special interactive reading group (compared to the children whose parents read in their usual fashion) were found to have more complex language in a number of different ways, a difference that was still present nine months later.

As children, we were all told to be quiet during reading at school and in libraries, and we may be tempted to pass on these rules to our very young children. However, if you are interested in facilitating your child's language and her comprehension of what she reads, talking with her while you read is very important.

Again, this should be a daily game you play with your child. You may find yourself tiring of the same books over and over again. Although you will want to introduce a new book occasionally, usually over your child's strong protests, repetition of the old books is very important to her. Just as you require many repetitions of a foreign word to master it, so does your child require many repetitions of words in her native language, which is still foreign to her in many respects. Repetition also is necessary in order to develop the routines that she will anticipate and in which she can participate proudly. These routines are the way in which she will develop a sense of the permanence of written language. In other words, as in the game of Expansions, repeated content allows her to shift her attention to form. So grit your teeth, and whip yourself into a state of wild enthusiasm for yet another reading of *Good Night Moon*.

If you begin to read even just one book every day to your twelve-month-old child, do you realize that by the time she enters kindergarten, she will have participated in almost 1,500 book-reading sessions with you? Two books a day, and that number will be almost 3,000. Such experience will be invaluable to her for many reasons. Some of the best memories children have of their parents are these book-reading times. In At Least One Book Every Day I noted that perhaps the single most important experience that predicts success in school is how much a child has been read to at home during early childhood.

✳ 4 ✳

Eighteen Months
to Two Years

Your child's recognizable vocabulary will expand dramatically at this age. No longer will you have to repeat words over and over again for him to pick them up. He will now absorb words after hearing them only a few times. Children seem to be particularly adept at picking up words you would rather they not know, so beware of what you say at this age. What you say today you will hear tomorrow. Children acquire words so fast at this age that it is called the "vocabulary explosion." Whereas at eighteen months most children have a productive vocabulary of up to fifty words, by the age of two years many children have over two hundred and fifty words in their vocabularies. Games such as Words and Things 2 and Can You, Must You, Could You, Would You? are aimed at increasing your child's vocabulary.

Your child's words will occur in the midst of a cloud of sounds that part from time to time to reveal a couple of recognizable words. He will be trying to make longer and longer statements, but the planning required to get a series of legitimate speech sounds correct is very difficult and will take more time.

A particular word may mean something different to a child

than to an adult. Between thirteen and thirty months, your child will tend to overuse words, calling not only bunnies but also dogs, birds, brushes, and soft blankets "bunny." Many children use "hot" not only to refer to hot things but also to refer to ice cubes, snow, and other cold things. Or they will use "up" to refer not only to wanting to be picked up but also to wanting to be put down.

Your child will tend to use single words where adults would use sentences. "Down" will mean "I want down from your lap." As he grows older, your child will become more complete in his speech even though he could continue to get what he wanted with his single words.

Sometimes your child will mean less than an adult means by certain words. For example, your child may use the word "car" only to refer to your family's red Volkswagen bug instead of to all cars. It takes a sharp ear to detect these overrestrictions in usage.

Your child will begin to combine words that he has regularly been using alone. He will say things like "Mo' mi'k," asking for more milk, and "Mo' tickle," asking you to tickle him some more. This is a very important advancement, though it still may be a challenge to you to figure out what he means by some of these early sentences. These early combinations have been called "telegraphic speech" because they consist only of important words, the few words necessary to get a point across. Your child has figured out these patterns because you have stressed them in your own speech.

Pronunciation of words will continue to differ from adult pronunciation. Some sounds are particularly difficult to learn. Many normal children do not master sounds like *t* or *ng* until they are six years old. Other sounds are not mastered until the age of seven or eight years. Normal two-year-olds have particular problems not only with these specific sounds but also with sequences of sounds in general.

Your child will understand more than he can spontaneously say, and imitate more than he can understand. Games encouraging imitation encourage language development. For this reason many of the games in this and the previous section are imitation games. Again, continue to play all the games you have learned so far.

At roughly this age, many children talk themselves to sleep. Such private conversation is filled with substitutions such as the ones noted by Stan Kuczaj, a researcher on such crib speech: " . . . I put Miss Piggy in back. I put bunny rabbit in back . . . " Kuczaj and others argue that substitutions are a way of practicing language. Language practice is very important because it allows the child to be in complete control over what is said and how it is said; such self-control maximizes the opportunity to engage in speech that is just new and different enough to be interesting and enjoyable to the child. Note, however, that some children rarely or never engage in crib speech, and they end up learning language perfectly well. Evidently, then, crib speech is only one form of language practice.

A number of researchers have found evidence that there are at least two distinctly different strategies that children adopt to learn language. These strategies become apparent usually by the time the child is nineteen months old. Katherine Nelson calls one strategy "referential." Children unconsciously using this strategy acquire large vocabularies early, mostly consisting of nouns. They frequently name objects and use language primarily to call attention to the objects and events in their environments. Nelson calls the other strategy "expressive." Children employing this strategy use pronouns rather than nouns ("I-do-dat"), repeat many formulaic phrases ("Gimme-dat"), and are much more imitative of large chunks of adult language than are referential children. Nelson provides us with evidence that children are influenced indirectly by their mothers' speech, and that this may be responsible for their adopting one or the other strategy. Mothers of referential children talk more about objects they name, while mothers of expressive children talk more about their children and other people.

Both strategies are successful ones. Referential and expressive children learn their language. But keep in mind that if your child resists playing imitative games, he may be doing so because he has a different strategy for learning language. Continue to give him the opportunity to play such games, but do not push them. Be especially responsive if your child initiates a round of a game he has refused to play earlier.

There are no dramatic emotional changes at this time, but there are common emotional issues, mostly involving separations of one sort or another. First of all, the issue of daily separation when the parent goes to work. Your child may very well continue to protest when you walk out that door. But now that he is a little older, he is capable of understanding more of what you say to him, so you have an option you did not have before. If at all possible, try to talk him into agreeing to your departure. One of the best ways of doing that is to buy a toy that he enjoys and let him play with it only when you are not there. For example, I bought my daughter Playdough and told her that if she stopped crying and let me go to work, she could play with her Playdough. In warmer weather, the lure was a sandbox. She was allowed to play with the sandbox only when I left. It took about five minutes every day to talk her into stopping crying and becoming interested in the Playdough or the sandbox, but it was well worth the time. I went to work feeling less anguish, and my daughter was much happier about the whole thing. Make sure the special toy is one your child really likes to play with and is a toy he will not tire of quickly.

Big separations: It is very common that children of this age have a sibling on the way. That will mean a hospital stay for their mother. With cesarean sections as common as they are, this could well involve a separation of a week or so. Or a parent has to go away on a business trip or to a professional convention for a week. Or parents decide that they need a two-week vacation because the child is no longer a baby. Or parents divorce, and the child will not see one parent or the other for perhaps months at a time.

How will a child of this age react to such prolonged separations? At first, he will protest his parents' departure in the same fashion as he does daily departures. He will cry vigorously, go to the door through which the parent departed, look for the lost parent, and reject a babysitter's efforts to comfort him.

Since we are talking about separations that continue, parents can expect that eventually their child will despair that his parents are never coming back. In this phase, he will no longer react vigorously to the separation. Instead, he will become listless, uncommunicative, whiny. He will be unresponsive, but no longer so rejecting of a babysitter's efforts to comfort him.

If parents return to find a child in the phase of protest or despair, they can expect that he will be upset with them, and he will show it primarily by being extraordinarily clingy. He needs extra attention for a while to be reassured that his parents are there for him.

Separations that continue longer eventually may trigger a detachment reaction from the child. Oddly enough, this will seem like a recovery. The child will become his old cheerful self. He will be interested in playing with toys again. The difference is seen when the child is reunited with his absent parents. Instead of being clingy, or even greeting them enthusiastically, he will ignore them.

In other words, when a child is upset, he will cry. If he is very upset, he will cry loudly and for a long time. But if he is subjected to a situation, such as prolonged separation, that is literally unbearably painful, he will express rage by silence, by ignoring. A parent will have to work very hard to regain his trust. It may take months, depending on a whole host of factors, including the child's age, how verbal he is (how much he can understand what is happening to him), how strong and secure his attachment was to the parent in the first place, and how attached he was to the babysitter.

For this reason, prolonged separations should be avoided whenever possible. If this is not possible, phone conversations and any other way of mitigating the separation should be employed. Perhaps much of the infamous sibling rivalry displayed upon a new baby's arrival home could be a reaction to the mother's seeming abandonment of a child rather than jealousy toward the new sibling.

In terms of cognitive development, this is the age when you

see a very dramatic development, what Piaget calls the invention of new means through mental combination. Put in simple terms, you will no longer be able to see everything your child is thinking. He will begin to solve simple problems in his head. For example, he will not solve puzzles simply by rubbing a piece back and forth over a hole. He can now look at a piece, look at a hole in the puzzle board, stop and think about it for a while, turn the piece so it fits, and place it nicely in the hole. Of course, he will not do this sort of thinking all the time, but the point is that he can do it. Or he will pull his wagon along the floor, get it stuck, and instead of simply continuing to tug at the wagon in a trial-and-error fashion, he may stand back, stop for a while and think about it, then lift the wagon out of the trap. This is quite a remarkable advancement.

He will also end up enjoying full-fledged hide-and-seek. He will be capable of hunting for things even in places in which he did not see them disappear.

Some children are more athletic than others and develop the ability to balance on one foot, to jump, and to pedal a tricycle. Others will do all these things a year from now. Again, it is even clearer at this age range than it was with infants that some children devote early energy to developing language at the expense of gross motor skills, while others do just the opposite. One little girl I knew could not ride a tricycle until just before her third birthday, but she was composing rather long sentences such as, "I want some more medicine on this booboo, Mommy" and "I hi'ed the big boy (waiter)" at twenty-two months. Another little boy was riding his bike at a little over two years, but he limited himself to saying things like "Mo' mi'k" until almost three.

This age is the best time to work on developing conversational skills, as in Keep the Ball Bouncing and Phone Talk. Duck Talk makes conversation particularly fun for your child. Games that you should play because of their importance in developing language and communication include Words and Things 2, Can You, Must You, Could You, Would You?, Keep the Ball Bouncing, and Phone Talk.

WORDS AND THINGS 2

Purpose

To teach your child categories of words.

Game

When your child is in the midst of his vocabulary explosion, teach him words in groups. You can talk to him about his stuffed animals, for example, or about things involved in the chores you are doing—cooking (food, pots and pans, dishes), doing laundry (names of clothes), gardening (names of utensils and plants), cleaning the cupboards. Or about body parts: "These are your eyes. You can blink your eyes and rub your eyes. You have one, two eyes. This is your nose. You can wiggle your nose and sniff with your nose. You have a very cute little nose and I have a big nose. And this is your mouth. You can smile with your mouth and pout with your mouth and shout with your mouth. These are your fingers. You have one, two, three, four, five fingers on each hand."

Variations

1. Reading such books as Richard Scarry's *Best Word Book Ever* (Golden Press), which includes many categories of pictures, is another good way of teaching groupings of things.

2. When you are sure that your child knows a word, deliberately use the wrong name in a teasing fashion and encourage him to correct you. If he knows what a cat and a duck are, for example, try pointing to a cat and saying something like, "That's a duck, isn't it? No, you say it's a cat? Well, I guess you are right after all."

CAN YOU, MUST YOU, COULD YOU, WOULD YOU?

Purpose

To keep conversation going by virtually ensuring your child's response and to highlight the complete form of verbs.

Game

When your child says, "Bad cat," say, "*Is* he a bad cat? Is he really?" When your child says, "Mi'k down," answer, "*Did* your milk fall down? It *did fall, did* it?" When your child says, "Hurt hand," answer, "*Have* you hurt your hand? You *have*?"

Variations

1. Questions that follow a comment of some sort serve the same function. For example, you might say something like, "You are putting all the blocks in the bucket, aren't you?" or "You petted the puppy very gently, didn't you?" or "You can climb all the way up the stairs, can't you?"

2. From time to time you can sing a little song made up of as many of the verbal auxiliaries as you can think of: Did you, must you, can you, do you, will you, have you, are you, may you, might you, were you, should you, shall you, could you, need you, dare you, don't you, can't you, won't you, haven't you, couldn't you, would you, wouldn't you? You can sing it all the way through or wait at the end of each question for your child's response.

Note

Whenever adults or children hear a list of words, they tend to remember the first words they hear. They also tend to remember the most recent words better than the words in the middle of the list, but the first words are remembered best of all. This phenomenon is so well documented in psychology that it has a special name—the primacy effect. Since your speech to a very young child will strike him as not much more than a list of words, what you habitually place at the front of your sentences will be important.

When you habitually say things like, "*Can* you do that?" or "*Did* you brush your teeth?" you give your child a helpful grammar lesson without even realizing it. Your child often can answer such questions with a simple yes or no. They may seem like pointless questions, whose only purpose is to keep the conversation going, since they usually repeat information that both you and your child know perfectly well. You may even feel that you would be insulting your child by asking questions with such obvious answers. Yet such questions place the verbal auxiliary ("can," "did," etc.) at the beginning of the sentence where your child will have a better chance of remembering it. Children whose parents frequently ask them such yes-or-no questions tend to acquire the verbal auxiliary before children whose parents do not.

KEEP THE BALL BOUNCING

Purpose

To encourage your child to take his turn in your conversations with him.

Game

As your child becomes more verbal at eighteen months or so, you will want to change the game of toddler talk to make it less one-sided. Let him begin to take turns. Don't just lecture him. On the other hand, remember that you do have to talk to your child to get him to talk to you. A good conversation is like volleying a tennis ball back and forth. The question is, how do you get your child to respond to you if he does not automatically do it?

The most basic strategy is to ask your child direct questions.

Ask specific, simple questions, such as, "I like ice cream, do you?" Some children will respond right away. But some won't. What then?

For one thing, pause after you say something. Just wait for your child to respond, keeping your eyes fixed on his. Wait longer than you would for an adult. Some parents repeat a number of the questions they ask their children just two seconds after having asked them the first time—not really giving their children much of a chance to respond.

If your child still does not respond to your question, even after you have waited for over five seconds for a response, simply repeat the question. Simple repetitions are more effective than other kinds of calls for attention in getting your child to pick up the conversational ball.

As your child grows older, you should ask real questions, questions to which you do not know the answer. Such questions are likely to get a response, and you may be surprised at how much your toddler knows.

If all else fails, ask your child permission to do something. The kind of question most likely to produce an appropriate response from your child is a request for permission from him. Parents who ask, "Can I sit in your chair?" or "Do you want me to help you put on your shirt?" or "May I watch you shampoo your own hair?" are offering an almost irresistible invitation to their children to respond. Such questions are answered appropriately by the child almost eighty percent of the time—more than any other type of question, provided the parent gives the child sufficient time to respond. Not all parents know this trick of asking permission from their children, and it is handy. I have seen an eighteen-month-old child who was stubbornly and repeatedly saying no to all his mother's demands that he take a bath suddenly turn charmingly compliant in response to his grandmother's asking, "Can I see you play alligator in your bath?" Incidentally, such requests for permission are in the form described in the game of Can You, Must You, Could You, Would You?, which turns out to have a good effect on language development.

By the time your child is two, if all goes well, most of your talk with him will be conversational.

Variation

Play a question-and-answer game that is the opposite of Mother May I. Ask your child if you can kiss him. Wait for his answer and respond to his wishes. Then ask him if you can touch him on his ear. Respond to his wishes. Ask him if you can tickle him. Respond to his wishes. And so forth.

Note

Although asking questions is a good way to get your child to talk to you, it is not a good way of getting your child to *do* what you want him to do. If you want your child to do something rather than talk back, put your request in command form. Instead of saying, "Would you put away your toys now?" say, "It is time to put away your toys now." The former would be a polite and effective way of asking an adult to do something, but it is a temptation for a tantrum to a child. It invites an expression of will from your child in the form of saying, "No!" He will think it unfair of you then to insist he do something you gave him a choice about doing.

DO WHAT I SAY

Purpose

To make following directions fun.

Game

When in any confined space (airport, doctor's office, bus station), give your child a series of directions, such as "clap your hands," and get him to follow them. Give him one direction at a time at first. If that is too easy, give two directions at a time. Most preschoolers will be able to follow about three directions at most. For example, you might say, "Touch your mouth, then make a fist, then stick out your tongue." Let your child do the actions as you say them, and increase or decrease the number of directions to hold his attention.

Variations

1. When you are in a more open space, you can adapt this game accordingly. Give your child directions on how to go to an imaginary zoo. For example, to get to the zoo, he might have to "go around the sandbox three times, go straight ahead to the end of the sidewalk, and turn left." This game became a favorite of my daughter's when she turned three. She began to ask me directions to the grocery store or chicken farm or grandmother's house herself. We even began to draw maps, at first in the sand, later on paper.

2. Switch roles; let your child give you directions.

Note

While occasional games of Do What I Say can be fun and an effective alternative to real discipline, directives in general are not effective as a means of facilitating language development. Many researchers have found that parents who rely upon directives as a means of communicating with their children have children who are less quick to acquire language than are children whose parents rely more upon questions and comments.

PHONE TALK

Purpose

To encourage imaginative play and familiarity with the rituals of conversation over the phone.

Props

Two play phones.

Game

Take a phone and give one to your child. Pretend to be an absent grandparent or parent and have a conversation with your child in that pretend role.

At first, just work on getting your child to say "hello"; "Can you say hello to Grandma? Say 'Hello, Grandma.' Good." Then work on "good-bye"; "You said hello very nicely. Now can you say 'Good-bye, good-bye, Grandma'?"

After your child engages in a number of "hello, good-bye" conversations, suggest things to talk about between the two—a recent snack, a new toy, something funny that the dog did: "Okay, you said hello just right. Now say 'I ate some oatmeal cookies.' Good." Use a different tone of voice to represent Grandma's answer. This part of the game gives your child practice in taking conversational turns.

Variations

1. Pretend to be an imaginary character such as Bert or Ernie or the Cookie Monster or Peter Rabbit or Santa Claus. Speak in an appropriate altered tone of voice.

2. Many parents encourage their children to talk to relatives. But instead of pawning your child off on some poor, unsuspecting relative who calls long distance to talk to you, call your child up yourself, perhaps from your office, and talk to him. You will have a much better chance than your relatives of understanding him over the phone, as well as of getting him to talk, since you know his routines. After a lot of real as well as pretend phone practice with you, *then* let your child talk to Grandma. Phone practice with you can save many expensive, embarrassingly long silences or garbled comments.

Note

This game is really a different version of Can You Say? and is useful for young children with real as well as pretend phone conversations. If you say to a two-year-old, "Tell your grandma about what happened to your puppy," you are likely to have the child merely say "puppy" to her grandmother, who, of course, will be left somewhat in the dark. Generally, the novelty of talking on a real phone will be sufficient to reduce your child's ability to speak. Give your young child a script of exactly what to say to get the conversation going. For example, tell your child, "Say 'Puppy spilled the garbage.'" You will be allowing him to perform on a level closer to his normal level.

DUCK TALK

Purpose

To introduce your child to different registers, or different ways of speaking.

Props

A duck toy or puppet can be used for this game. Variation 1 requires the cardboard tube from inside paper towels or gift wrap. Other variations could be devised using anything else that makes your voice sound different.

Game

To create an appropriate "duck" voice, pinch your nose closed and talk to your child. Introduce yourself as a duck. Tell him about how you like to swim, how you like to play with the frogs, how you are "quackers" about going to your duck pond, and so forth. Children find the high-pitched, nasal cartoon voice that comes out of your mouth when you talk with your nose closed very funny.

Variations

1. Talk through the cardboard tube in a deep, booming voice, but be careful not to hurt your child's ear by pointing the tube too close to it.

2. As your child grows older, he will want to take a turn talking funny. Pinch your child's nose closed and get him to talk like a duck or give him a chance to talk through the "megaphone."

A B SOUP

Purpose

To teach your child the alphabet.

Props

One of the many alphabet books on the market. For children this age, I would recommend that you purchase a cloth or thick board book, as it will get a lot of use from still clumsy little hands. My favorite one is a cloth alphabet book with several pictures for each letter. This book is useful for a long time, for children who are starting to read as well as for children in the age range we are considering. For older, preschool children, who know how to use books without ripping them, there are beautifully illustrated alphabet books available. At last count, I had a half-dozen different ones around the house.

The variations below also require a set of plastic letters (2), a pencil, magic marker, and paper (3), and an alphabet plate, cup, or placemat (5).

Game

Take one capital letter each day and teach your child the name of it. Talk about it. Say things like, "This is an *A* (point to *A* in the book). Can you say 'A'? Good. A is for Apple (point to picture of apple)."

Now pick up an old magazine and point out a number of different A's. Take a walk with your child and show him some more A's. Eventually, if your child is truly ready for the game, he will take over and begin pointing out As to you. Of course, be enthusiastic if he correctly identifies the letters, but only mildly corrective if he, say, confuses M's and N's for a while. In the latter event, say things like, "Well, you are close. That's actually an N."

Variations

1. Of course, the old favorite, the alphabet song, is probably the most common version of this game. The song goes:

> A, B, C, D, E, F, G,
> H, I, J, K, L, M, N, O, P.
> Q, R, S,
> T, U, V.
> W, X, Y, and Z.
> Now you know your ABC's.
> Now you sing them after me.

2. Buy a set of plastic magnetic letters (there are many different sets available in any toy store). Put them on your refrigerator. Ask your child to find particular letters that he knows.

3. Have your child scribble a picture with a pencil. With a contrasting magic marker, trace over the X or the O or the T that he has inadvertently drawn. Eventually, he will want to deliberately try to make the letters himself. Let him decide when he wants to try that, however.

4. As you are riding in the car, ask your child if he sees any letters. My daughter loved this variation. She would proudly announce that she had spotted a B on a billboard or an S in a stop sign.

5. Give your child a place setting or placemat decorated with

the alphabet. My daughter picked out such a placemat when she was two and has used it ever since. During at least one or two meals she drills herself on the alphabet. It has evolved into an opportunity to play the Words That Begin with *B* game.

6. Serve your child alphabet soup or alphabet spaghetti. Talk about the letters he eats.

Note

My daughter gave me the title for this game. When she was almost two, she continually requested A B soup for lunch, not because of its wonderful taste, but because she delighted in telling me the names of letters she knew and in asking me the names of letters she did not know. She led the drill, in other words. And that is the most important thing to keep in mind. While some children are ready to play this game and its infinite variations now, others will not be ready for a couple of years. Do not push your child to play this game. Before the days of *Sesame Street*, which drills the alphabet on every show, children rarely used to learn the alphabet before the age of five. There is plenty of time, and while this is an important language game for working on reading skills, it is not the only one nor even the most important one, despite its fame.

✳ 5 ✳

Two to Three Years

By the age of two, your child will be a much more exciting conversationalist than she was before. Much of your interchange will be conversational, whereas before you had to do the greater share of talking. Your child will be using more and more complete sentences of increasing complexity.

For example, a child about two years old produced the following conversation:

> MOTHER: What did you do today?
> CHILD: Play farm. Play frog. Play Alice.
> MOTHER: What else did you do? What did you eat?
> CHILD: A beans. (Pause) Some (pause) beans. Some (pause) Cokes.

At three years, the same child's average conversation was far too lengthy to include in a book of this scope.

What will make your two-year-old's conversation truly interesting is that she will begin to talk about things that happened previously as well as abstract things such as feelings. For example, one two-year-old I know rather regularly began to say, "I scared." She also declared her love for her friend: "My Alex is the best friend of mine. I can hold hands with him and pat him."

Your child will begin to make up things, especially if encouraged to do so. At two and a half, she may develop an imaginary companion—about one in five children do so. Such imaginary companions are topics for lively, imaginative exchanges, and many parents find it fun to play along with their children. Your child's increased ability to talk about distant events and abstractions and to be imaginative is capitalized upon in Red and Round and Happy; Slowly, Quickly; Over, Under, Around, and Through; Remember; Pretend; and What If?

Your child will still be working on pronunciation. A typical two-year-old said "lello" for "yellow," "lucky" for "yucky," "mugit" for "music," "some ba milk" for "a bottle of milk," "solf" for "salt," "mell it" for "smell it," "pido" for "pillow," "hornk" for "horn," and "prensents" for "presents." New words are mapped on to the sound of old words. That two-year-old called her swimming suit a "swimming soup," for example. By the age of three, these endearing mispronunciations had disappeared, though she still said "amidals" for "animals," "prensents" for "presents," "I'm firsty" for "I'm thirsty," and "Come wis me" for "Come with me." Her parents had done nothing to correct her pronunciation during this time other than to use the correct pronunciation of the words in question and to seek clarification of things she said that they did not understand.

Your child also will still be working on the meaning of words. One researcher estimates that between two and four years of age, children learn several new words a day. Children at this age also are filling out the meaning of words they already use perfectly well. For example, two-year-olds' infamous negativism may be at least in part the result of an incomplete understanding of the word "no." Two-year-olds have heard their parents respond with a sharp "no" far more often than they respond "yes," so "no" may come to mean something like "what to say in response to anything" rather than its true negative meaning. In fact, in response to things like "Do you want an ice cream cone?" you often can observe two-year-olds imitating their parents by saying "no" quite adamantly and with a furrowed brow, followed two seconds later by an eager reach for the cone.

A two-year-old will say things like, "I wanta see it" when he really means, "I want to touch it," a difference of definition that can lead to a long, frustrating series of replies, "But you *are* seeing it," unless the parent is tuned into what the child really means to say.

It is during this time that your child will also figure out how to use pronouns. At age two, my daughter quite regularly said "I carry you" when she wanted us to carry her, but she sorted it out within the year. Again, you do not need to explain the rules to your child. Imagine trying to say "Say 'you' when you mean 'me,' and 'me' when you mean 'you.'" By using language properly yourself and playing the Can You Say? 2 game with your child, things should go smoothly.

Towards the end of this year, your child may develop some rather complex sentences such as "I needa finish my egg," or "I want to read that book," or "I want to see the waffles cooking," or "Let me find it for you. Sit right there and talk."

Many children master the alphabet song during this age period and begin to work on recognizing the letters and even associating characteristic sounds with them. *Sesame Street* has made most children prodigies in this regard, learning the alphabet well before their parents did.

Less is known about different strategies for learning language at this time than earlier on, but individual differences in the energy put into language learning continue. One two-year-old's average statement might be something like the length of "I missed it" or "I not crabby," while another's might be more like the length of "Hi, mama."

Language is seen as a window into thought processes, or intelligence, and tests exist for assessing individual differences in preschoolers' intelligence. However, such tests are neither necessary nor desirable for most children during this time. Intelligence test scores are not generally considered predictive until the age of six years anyway, and some research has found a great deal of fluctuation even after that point. One study found that many children change dramatically on the IQ scale between the ages of two and a half and seventeen years of age. A young child who scored in the slow learner range may score in the average range as an adolescent, or a six-year-old child who scored in the average range may score in the gifted range as an adolescent.

The only good reasons for giving young children intelligence tests at this time would be to do psychological research or to assess children who seem to lag behind their peers. In other words, the only reason you should consider having your child tested is if you suspect that she is having unusual difficulty learning language. By unusual difficulty at this time, I mean that she seems to understand very little of what you say to her and/or that she produces almost no words at all. Some children do not develop language until after two years of age, for no apparent reason. Some do not develop language at the usual rate because they primarily talk to other children and watch television, both of which are not adequate for normal language development. Some children do not develop language normally because they have a hearing impairment or a problem with processing language. Some children do not develop language because they have more profound mental or emotional difficulties that would require the attention of medical and psychological professionals.

For most children and most parents, however, it probably would be better if intelligence tests had never been invented. Then parents could truly just relax and enjoy their children. Many psychologists feel that contemporary parents are pushing their children too much to become highly accomplished writers or artists or dancers or musicians or athletes at too young an age. Psychologists are seeing such children because so many seem burned out, depressed, suicidal, or otherwise disturbed. Children may react to such pressure in a variety of ways—by rejecting the idea of achieving great things, or by trying to become an adult in other ways, such as by drinking or precociously engaging in sexual relations.

Children will and should be allowed to develop language and other skills in their own time. They will do a better job if they are not pressured in this development.

Emotional issues between two and three years of age are well known. After all, we are talking about the infamous Terrible Twos. Your child will want to do things for herself. She will want to set her own goals. She will reject your offerings of food and toys, often seemingly just for the sake of rejection, not because she genuinely dislikes the food or toys offered.

And, of course, this is the age of outrageous temper tantrums. Your child will prostrate herself in the grocery store, screaming, flopping around, even perhaps banging her head on the floor because you refuse to buy her a box of Fruit Loops. Once in progress, there is nothing you can do to stop a tantrum. Spanking will escalate your difficulties. So will yelling; she will simply yell louder. Pleading is ineffectual. Giving in to the child's demands will give her the message that tantrums are a good way to get what she wants, so she will be much more likely to use that technique in the future. Instead of all these understandable but inadvisable responses, you should see that she does not hurt herself or others and then ignore her until she rides out the tantrum.

Are all parents, then, doomed to public humiliation during this time? The answer is yes and no. What you *can* do about temper tantrums is prevent most of them. And you can do this primarily by distracting your child. A number of the games in the following section were inspired by grocery shopping or traveling with my daughter when she was two. Distraction was such a reliable way of preventing her tantrums that she really never had any tantrums in public after I learned what kinds of situations triggered a tantrum for her and invented the games in this section. She would have a tantrum after this point only when we were at home and I was too lazy or too slow to play one of the games with her. What triggered tantrums for her, and what does so for many children, is wanting something they should not play with or that you do not want them to have. A language game begun fast enough can make them forget all about the "forbidden fruit."

Should distraction fail, many parents resort to offering their child a cookie if they behave themselves. Other parents may feel qualms about such obvious bribery, but with young children it is by far the most preferable tactic available for controlling behavior.

The alternatives are ignoring bad behavior, nagging the child to do what you want, or spanking or other punishment for bad behavior. None of these alternatives seems very desirable, and there is a lot of evidence that they are not nearly so effective as the use of rewards for good behavior.

The question of rewards should be rephrased: What kind of rewards are the best ones to use? It is well known in psychology that rats, children, and many other species will perform a less desirable activity if they are allowed the chance to perform a more desirable one. Most of your tussles with your two-year-old will boil down to your wanting her to do something and her wanting to do something else at that particular time. Often that something else is not really bad in itself, just inconveniently timed. Allow her to do what she wants to do *after* she does what you want her to do. In other words, children will frequently suggest their own best reward.

Cognitive development is a matter of improving the ability to represent things symbolically that began during the previous age range. Your child's language, as I have already mentioned, is reflective of this enhanced ability. At about two and a half, some children begin to name a few colors correctly. Most two-year-olds know that they are a girl or a boy, though they may think they can grow up to be the opposite sex.

During this time, your child's cognitive and emotional growth will take place in the context of play. Most (but by no means all) parents naturally engage in at least some fantasy play with their children, perhaps at their child's insistence. Like many parents, you may find such play fun. However, you may not be aware of how important play is to your child's developing emotions and thought. Erik Erikson and other clinicians argue that children attempt to master emotional issues, such as separation anxiety, by acting them out in play. Jean Piaget argues that play is the primary mechanism of cognitive development. Children come to know objects and situations in play by interpreting the unfamiliar in terms of the familiar and by exploring the new things that can be done with unfamiliar ones. Jerome Bruner points out that children at first assemble small pieces of larger acts in play, going on to combine these into higher-order skills. Other psychologists have examined the ways in which play fosters problem-solving of all sorts.

Creativity often is measured by seeing how many uses people can think of for a paper clip, for example. Fantasy play directly encourages creativity by involving the exploration of new things to do with old objects. While at two or three years, children tend to stick fairly close to the reality of a situation or object, they will become more imaginative with age, departing more and more from the real functions of things in their actions with them.

Play has been called the "zone of potential development," because pretend reading is a precursor for real reading, pretend writing for real writing, and so forth. In fact, encouraging an older child to "pretend to be best friends" with a sibling, for example, may provide her with an arena in which to work that into a reality.

Physical development, like cognitive development during this time, is a matter of getting better and better, doing more and more things. But nothing seems as dramatic as it did earlier, when your child's first steps were worthy of long-distance phone calls and the like.

The games that I invented to distract my child from temper tantrums are What If?, Corky, Shy Finger and Rude Duck, and Don't You Ever Try to Tickle a Pickle. The rest of the games in this section are critical to various aspects of your child's language development, especially What Did You Say, Dear?, Remember, Pretend, and Once Upon a Time.

WHAT DID YOU SAY, DEAR?

Purpose

To let your child know gently when she has not said something clearly enough for you to understand.

Game

When your child says something that you do not understand for any reason, be sure to ask questions until you do understand what she is saying. If she says something like, "I went ashide," you might respond, "You went where?" If she says, "Ashide," take a guess: "Oh, you went *outside*? Yes, you did go outside, didn't you?"

Variation

Switch roles. Encourage your child to seek clarification from you if you have not spoken clearly enough. The temptation for parents confronted by repeated "what's" from their two-year-old is frustration, unfortunately. But if parents can set this emotion aside, they are giving their child a lesson that even though communication takes work, it eventually will be successful provided both parties continue to try.

Note

Most adults become so embarrassed or exasperated when one or two attempts to convey a message to another adult fail that they tend to let the matter drop. If you ask someone to repeat a message twice and you still do not understand, you might well find yourself smiling and nodding and hoping for the best rather than asking the other person to repeat himself again. Too many requests for communication from other adults may seem rude.

When the situation is reversed, and, let's say, someone who is hard of hearing continues to ask you to repeat some offhand remark, you may (a) become mortified that you ever said anything so inane that it makes you cringe the third time you repeat it, (b) unfairly accuse your listener of not trying to hear, or (c) give up and change your response so that your listener can understand you.

These adult sensibilities truly may impede communicating with two-year-olds. Children are not so touchy about being asked to repeat themselves, nor do they seem flustered by repeatedly asking the same question of adults. I have known children to repeat a question twenty times when their parents are talking to someone else on the phone, for example. They seem quite prepared to put up with frustration in the interest of eventual communication.

However, I have also known adults who confessed that they smiled and nodded their way through most of their conversations with children who were difficult to understand. I suspect that the children became dissatisfied with such irrelevant responses after a while. I also do not see how the children could speak more clearly unless they were given information about when they were not clear as opposed to when they were.

Important recent research by Catherine Snow and others documents the fact that many mothers respond to most poorly formed statements by two-year-olds with requests for clarification. How can anyone get better at communicating unless they do not know that they have failed?

One caveat, however. While some parents do not seek clarification enough, others may overdo this. Some cases have been documented of parents who never do anything but echo their children by way of seeking clarification. It is wise to beware of such rigid rituals. Occasionally accepting what a child says that you are pretty sure you understand is important too. Furthermore, extending the topic of conversation is essential if you want your child to become an enjoyable conversational partner.

CAN YOU SAY? 2

Purpose

To develop the complexity of your child's language.

Game

Read a poem such as "Custard the Dragon" or "Alligator Pie" or any of the many Mother Goose rhymes or A. A. Milne verses line by line to your child and have her repeat the lines. Do this over and over again with the same poem and encourage your child to memorize it.

Variation

At appropriate times during conversations, quote poems or stories that are familiar to your child. Weaving what is said in books with what happens in life shows your child the use of books, as well as your appreciation for well-crafted language.

Note

Memorizing poetry has gone out of fashion in schools, probably in reaction to overemphasis on such exercises in the past, but memorizing at least some good poems and prose is still a fine way to establish some patterns of good speaking.

Your child will imitate aspects of language that she has begun to understand. For example, by playing this game frequently while you read to her, you may help her to develop the ability to use auxiliary verbs and pronouns. However, this is a game that can be played at different levels throughout life.

Notice that your child is not a tape recorder. You cannot just push a button and get her to imitate you. Even at this more advanced stage, sometimes she will imitate you on demand, sometimes she will not. Do not push too hard to play this game. Neither you nor your child will enjoy it if you do. But if you are both in the mood for it, it can be fun; it is a time-honored, basic means of language acquisition.

RED AND ROUND AND HAPPY

Purpose

To teach your child words for abstract or invisible things.

Props

Assorted toys, a clock with hands, and an hourglass.

Game

Talk about abstractions such as colors, shapes, emotions, and time in terms of concrete objects. Once your child knows the names of fruits and animals and toys, you can name and point out a "yellow banana, a yellow bandana, a yellow duck, and a yellow truck" all at one time. Or a "square napkin, square block, square window, square chair," etc. Or a "happy, smiling clown, a happy face, and a happy mommy." Numbers can be talked about in terms of "one, two, three, four, five apples, and one, two, three, four, five blocks, and one, two, three, four, five stairs."

Act out emotions. Really ham up being sad or mad or glad or bad, making exaggerated expressions of these emotions. At first label the emotions repeatedly. When your child knows the labels, ask her what emotion you are pretending. Eventually you can go on to ask why she thinks a person would feel that way. Our daughter went on to request that we act "sad. Now glad. Mad. Bad."

Time can begin to be talked about in terms of "I want you to wait till all the sands go through that hole and end up on the bottom of the hourglass before you get up from your nap" or "Daddy will be home in the time it takes for the little hand on the clock to move from here to there" or "Grandma will be coming to visit us in the time it·takes for you to have three nights' sleep" or "We will be at the ocean in the time it takes for us to play one game

of Big Girls, one game of Can You Say?, and to make up five
stories."

Variations

1. Once your child knows at least some colors and shapes, for
example, be sure to play rounds of Test Questions with her: "Is
this ball red or blue?" "Is this a square board or a round one?"
2. Once you have talked about a set of abstractions for a
while, bring together a group of things, all but one of which are
alike in some way, and ask your child, "Which one is different?"
For example, group together a blue shoe, a blue block, a blue truck,
a blue book, and a yellow duck and ask your child which one is
different. Or group together a ball, a steering wheel, a paper plate,
a plastic ring, and a square block and ask which one is different.
Or draw several different kinds of sad faces (a clown, a boy, a girl,
a cat) and a happy one and ask which one is different. After your
child has identified correctly which one is different, ask her how
all the other objects are the same.

SLOWLY, QUICKLY

Purpose

To draw your child's attention to adverbs.

Game

Go through the following action sequences with your child. You
do the action first, then ask your child to imitate you. Do more
than the suggested actions for any one adverb comparison. Go on
to another set of adverbs when your child tires of the first set. Use
other adverb comparisons.

Walk slowly. Now walk quickly.
Talk slowly. Now talk quickly.

Walk loudly. Now walk softly.
Talk loudly. Now talk softly.

Put this ball down gently. Now put the ball down roughly.
Pet your kangaroo gently. Now pet that kangaroo roughly.

Draw a line smoothly. Now draw a line roughly.

Pull that wagon smoothly. Now pull that wagon roughly.

Stack those blocks up carefully. Now stack them up messily.
Put these spoons in the drawer carefully. Now put them in
messily (toss spoons in carelessly).

Run nicely (jog carefully, arms at side). Now run wildly (flail
arms, run very fast and hard, bump into soft cushions, etc.).

Dance nicely. Now dance wildly.

Variation

Instead of the standard adverb, use comparison phrases such as,
"Stretch like a cat. Now run like a horse. Sniff like a mouse. Now
waddle like a duck."

Note

Knowledge of these adverbs obviously has a payoff for you. You
will be able to control your child much more easily if she knows
how to speak "softly," lay things down "gently," and so forth.

OVER, UNDER, AROUND,
AND THROUGH

Purpose

To extend your child's knowledge of prepositions.

Props

A small car and a basket, or comparable items.

Game

Give your child the car. You hold the basket and ask your child to
make the car drive through the hoop. Have the child drive it over,
under, around, beside, behind, in front of, into and out of the
basket. Act out with your hands any prepositions your child does
not know. Try at least one that she does not know, but do not try
too many new ones at one time.

Variation

Get your child to hold the basket and give you directions for
driving the car. Ask questions if she runs out of ideas: "Would you
like me to drive the car underneath the basket?"

Note

You should play this game only when your child knows some
prepositions, like "in" and "out." This game will work only for a
short time with children who do not know many prepositions.
Work on teaching your child one preposition per session. This
game is a good one to play while driving with your child, because
you can talk about how you are driving *over* rivers, how the rivers
are *under* you and you are going *through* tunnels, etc.

REMEMBER

Purpose

To improve your child's memory for specific events, as well as to develop her memory skills in general.

Props

A photograph album filled with shots of family events is a good occasional prompt for remembering events and people.

Game

Although you are not likely to get a very accurate or complete answer from your two-year-old, you should begin to ask her to remember events that happened months prior to your questioning. This interchange between a twenty-nine-month-old girl and her mother is an example of the kind of interviewing that is most effective with two-year-olds:

> ADULT: I was remembering yesterday when we had lunch in the car because it was too cold out. And then we got all bundled up and where did we go?
> CHILD: Home.
> ADULT: We went to see the house.
> CHILD: Where is it?
> ADULT: Remember when we went to Cook's Forest?
> CHILD: Yeah. Are we going now.
> ADULT: No, it's a long drive. We just went yesterday. How did you go to the house? Did you walk?
> CHILD: No.
> ADULT: How did you go?
> CHILD: I, on a sled.
> ADULT: Un huh. Were you cozy?
> CHILD: Yeah.

ADULT: What did we wrap around you?
CHILD: A blanket.
ADULT: Did anything happen to you while we were pulling the toboggan?
CHILD: Yeah, I tipped over.
ADULT: What happened?
CHILD: I felled off.
ADULT: And then what did we do?
CHILD: Goed in the car.
ADULT: We put you back on. We shook the blanket out. . . .

Ask your child open-ended questions like, "Remember what we did yesterday?" to begin with. If she does not remember anything, ask her more specific questions like the mother did above: "Where did we go?" If, as in the case above, the child does not give the right answer, you may supply it yourself (they went to see the vacation house they own rather than back home). However, it is wise to avoid overt corrections like, "No, that's not where we went."

Variation

Ask your child to help plan things with you. Ask her to remember one or two items to buy at the grocery store, for example.

Note

Two-year-olds will not contribute very much to the family narrative, but do not let this lack of responsiveness make you stop asking them to remember events that happened long ago. Some recent research indicates a strong relationship between the number of questions mothers ask their two-year-olds about relatively distant events and their children's general ability to recall things by the time they are three, just one year later. Memory skills are crucial to school performance, and you will give your child quite a headstart in remembering things simply by frequently asking her to do so even before she seems ready.

In my research with Carole Peterson, we found striking differences in the way in which parents interviewed their children about past experiences, shared and unshared. Some parents, like the one in the example above, literally do not take "no" for an answer to questions like, "What did you do at school today?" Other parents respond to their two-year-olds' inability to contribute much to the joint reminiscence by switching the topic of conversation. Evidently these parents misread the inability of two-year-olds to remember very much about what happened as the reluctance of some adults to recall an experience upon occasion. In any case, parents who extended discussion of one past event by asking questions, making statements, and seeking clarification about whatever their child *did* say had children who told long, beautifully developed narratives at the age of six. Parents who switched topics frequently on their two-year-olds, instead of extending these topics, had children who told very brief narratives or not many narratives at all four years later. There were still other parents who extended their children's narratives by correcting virtually everything their children said. Children of such parents may develop the ability to tell a good story. However, they may decide not to tell their stories to their parents. The little boy in our study whose parents did this the most eventually responded to their invitation to recall something with the refrain, "You tell me."

There is a myth that some children are "born storytellers." But the Myth of the Born Storyteller is just that—a myth. Children of school age who tell good stories have had at least one parent who knew how to interview them and did so daily, beginning somewhere around the age of two years. Paradoxically, if you persist in asking questions of your child at two, you may not have to do so as much later on.

PRETEND

Purpose

To encourage your child's imagination and to develop language, thinking, social role-playing, and emotional problem-solving.

Props

Your child's toys.

Game

Construct imaginary episodes using your child's toys. Comment on toys that are present. Say such things as, "Is that bear mad at you?" or "That doll is a scuba diver" or "Is that (play) stove hot?"

Talk about imaginary objects that are often associated with those toys. Say, "This (pretend) soup is ready; would you like some?"

Ask your child to extend the fantasy. Say, "What do you think Pooh Bear wants for supper?" or "Where should we put the (play) barn?"

If your child comes up with a fantasy action, describe it. Say, "You're putting the dolly in her bed, aren't you?" If your child comes up with a fantasy comment, repeat it. If your child says, "Soup hot," reply, "Yes, the soup is very hot, isn't it?"

Variations

1. With children who readily play fantasy games, use puppets. Give yourself and your child a puppet and have them talk back and forth. You can develop some very nice plays this way.

2. When your child wants something she does not have or has lost, tell her to pretend that something else is the desired object. Make suggestions. A stick can serve as a horse, a ribbon or shoelace or popcorn strung together can serve as necklaces. As she grows older, your child may grow fussier about what will do as a substitute, but encourage her imagination anyway. She will eventually become more willing to be imaginative again. If you consistently encourage pretending, not only will you foster her skill in metaphor (see Metaphor Games, pp. 151–154), but you will give your child the freedom to fulfill her wishes. An imagination is worth far more than the most expensive toy you can buy.

WHAT IF?

Purpose

To encourage your child's imagination.

Game

Ask your child such questions as the following:
"What if I put a banana on your head?" Wait for a response.
"What if I put some earrings on the Pilsbury Doughboy?"
"Well, what if I put you in a big bowl of Jell-O?"
"What if I bought all the cereal in this aisle and took it home and put it in your bedroom?"
"What if we filled up the whole grocery store with balloons?"
"What if elephants wore pajamas?"
"What if we put a bear in Daddy's slippers?"
"What if we found a bulldozer in the frozen food section?"
"What if we gave the carrots a bubble bath?"
Make up other questions. Be sure to mention things that your child is interested in. Note that it is easier to look around you and imagine something funny happening to something right in front of you at the time and then walk away from the immediate scene. Younger children will probably not say too much beyond "yes" or "no" in response to your wild imaginings, but older children on their own may begin to come up with some of the consequences of having, say, an elephant in the pickles. If your child says "no" to one of your suggestions, move on to another one. Ham it up. Do not just stick with a plain old bulldozer in the frozen food section. Make it a big, mean, purple bulldozer, for example.
Once a child says "yes," you can extend the game: "What if I put a giraffe on your shoulder?"
Child: "Yes."
"Okay, here's the giraffe. It is a nice little baby giraffe, with a long, long neck (make gesture showing long neck on top of child's shoulder). This giraffe is yellow with spots on him. Would you like to pet this giraffe?"

Variation

As your child grows older (three, four, five years and up) and plays this game well, switch to a more sophisticated version called Imagine. Ask your child to imagine that she is on a desert island; ask her what she would bring and what she would do with her time. Or ask her to imagine that she is on the moon; ask her what she would see and feel and smell and hear. Or ask her to imagine that she lived in the days of the cave men and women; what would she do if she saw a family of hungry cave people from a different tribe stealing from her tribe's food cave?

Note

What If? is a great distraction game to play in places like the grocery store in order to ward off a tantrum from your "terrible" two-year-old, who is apt to prostrate herself on the ground unless you let her open a bag of potato chips—or you think of something else quickly.

What If? and Imagine are limited to the extent that parents' imaginations are limited. Parents may find their own imaginations a little rusty and in need of practice when they start to play this game.

CORKY

Purpose

To encourage your child's imagination.

Props

A felt-tip pen and whatever object is close at hand and defaceable, such as a cork, a paper napkin or towel, a paper bag, a piece of paper folded into a triangle, or your own hand.

Game

With the felt-tip pen, draw a face on a cork or your own hand (eyes on the index finger and mouth on your thumb) or some other object. Make it distinctive in some way—especially pretty or mean or silly. For example, you might draw a pretty face on the cork and make it talk in a high voice, commenting on the day's activities. Use it like a puppet. Name it, in this case, Corquette. Have it act out what your family did. "Ooooo. Did you see that beautiful dog with the brown and white spots? Wasn't it lovely? Did you see it running back and forth (Corquette can be chasing a napkin here). And didn't you like that little boy who was playing with trucks? He was nice."

Or how about the silly napkin clown, Goopy? Goopy has magic marker eyes and a lipstick nose and mouth and consists of half a napkin stuffed with the other half of the same napkin. Goopy sounds silly and does things like falling off the table: "Duhh, I guess I slipped, didn't I? That was silly." Goopy sits down in some water and gets all wet: "Gee, I guess I'm all wet, aren't I? That's silly, isn't it?" Or Goopy accidentally gets all tangled up in your child's shoestrings and has a hard time getting out: "Golly. I'm all wrapped up. I don't know how I got into this mess. Guess I'll have to ask you to help me out." And so forth.

A new character can always appear if the old one doesn't work or becomes boring.

Variation

On rainy days, more permanent characters can be made at home out of socks, for example. There are hundreds of patterns around for making cute puppets, but you really do not need a pattern. Ask your child to suggest what to use for eyes, nose, mouth, etc. Ask your child what the puppet's name is and what he or she is like.

Note

Although puppets are nothing new (any toy store will have some), the idea of giving each puppet a distinctive voice and character may be new to you. You can introduce your child to the idea of registers, or different ways of speaking—like a baby, like a grown-up, etc. The appearance of the puppet matters far less than the language games a parent plays with it. The cutest puppet in the world is no fun for a two-year-old unless a parent's hand inhabits it. And, as this game capitalizes on, a makeshift puppet can be fascinating if the language games played with it are good.

So why is this game named Corky? Corky made his appearance one evening at a restaurant when my daughter was hungry and tired of waiting for food and bored with the toys we had brought along as distractions. Corky turned out to be quite a rascal, jumping into water glasses, playing with a knife, grabbing sugar packets, doing all sorts of expressly forbidden things. We had been reprimanding our daughter for doing much the same thing before Corky arrived. Now she reprimanded him—a much more pleasant situation. I highly recommend this game to anyone in a similar position.

SHY FINGER AND RUDE DUCK

Purpose

To ward off temper tantrums and to encourage imaginative play.

Props

Your hand.

Game

In the last game, I suggested a number of dispensable materials that can be turned into puppets. But I often have found my two-year-old on her way to a tantrum in the grocery store, for example, where I cannot make a puppet fast enough. Except out of my hands. So one day, the Shy Finger was born. This was a whispering finger (my index finger) who was quite frightened of loud talking or crying. My daughter immediately quieted down to hear what the Shy Finger had to say and to hide him from all the scary noises of the outside world.

When my daughter was bored, the Rude Duck sometimes emerged. The Rude Duck simply involved my hand imitating a duck bill and me imitating a harsh-spoken duck who did naughty things like trying to bite the Shy Finger or splash water in a mall water fountain. Like Corky in the previous game, the Rude Duck often needed to have my daughter discipline him.

A third character for all occasions is the Sad Spider, with my hand imitating the legs of a spider and me imitating some weird crying. My daughter loved to comfort this spider. Sometimes she was so successful that the spider became playful and tickled her.

All of these characters have prevented countless numbers of tantrums from happening by successfully distracting my daughter. I should mention that they have been so successful that I often grew tired of the game before she did, but by that time, we had checked out of the supermarket or arrived at our destination or gotten into the doctor's office after all—some place where there were new distractions.

Variation

Encourage your child to have a hand puppet that makes frequent visits. My daughter soon had the Sad Spider and the Rude Duck puppet in her repertoire.

ONCE UPON A TIME

Purpose

To familiarize your child with the structure of a story and to encourage creativity.

Game

Take turns in making up a story about some object in sight, like a bird or a toy or a bulldozer. For example, point out a helicopter and say, "Once upon a time, a little boy named Ted (your child's name) took that helicopter to New York to visit his Uncle Bill. What did he do there?" Your child might reply that he "went to MacDonald's. Had a Big Mac and Coke."

You continue the story by suggesting that the Big Mac was so big that the little boy kept eating and eating it but he couldn't finish it. "Then what did he do?" Wait for your child's response, incorporate it into the story somehow, and continue until together you have made a good story.

Or begin a story about a toy cat. "Once upon a time, Cat lived in Italy, which is along ways away. I bet he told you what he did there, didn't he?"

"He eated mouses."

"Oh, you say he ate mice. Did he ever try to catch the King Mouse?"

"Yes, he did. He chase him. Down the tracks." And so forth.

Variation

Encourage your child to tell you a pretend story all by himself.

Note

This game differs from Pretend in that you are not going to act out everything in the story, and your goal is to make a well-informed tale with a beginning, a middle, and an end (see Tell a Story to Get a Story, pp. 117–121).

JOKER

Purpose

To show your child how much you enjoy what she has to say and to work on the idea of fixed language, which will be an important component of understanding written language.

Game

Two-year-olds say funny things, at first without intending to do so. But when they discover the laughter they provoke from their parents, they will enjoy repeating these things. The only problem is that they do not necessarily remember their own "jokes." So one language game you can play is to remember something funny that your child has said and ask her to repeat it in the future. At first, you will probably have to whisper the whole thing to her, announcing to the crowd that she has a joke for them. After practice, she will need only an abbreviated prompt.

My joke collection from two-year-olds includes the following. One little boy would say "broccoli" at odd times, without any broccoli or even any food present. It's really pretty funny. A little two-year-old girl decided one day that "I scared of the three" in the pool, while swimming. She was in her mother's arms at the time, smiling, and not, in fact, acting scared. When asked, "Are you telling me another one of your jokes?" the little girl claimed that she now was scared of her doll, and of a nearby chair, and of her Aunt Susie, and so forth, laughing shortly after I laughed each time she mentioned a new "scare." (I am *not* recommending making fun of genuine feelings, but in this case the child clearly was not scared. After that, it became a routine.) That same girl, Dora, was talking to herself one day, while I was in the room, when she discovered a joke that was also a principle of language: "Ma*ma*, Mom*mie*, Da*da*, Dad*die*, Dora, Dor*rie*." She paused, turned to her babysitter, Lisa, and said, "Li*sa*, Li*sie*!" The laugh she got prompted many repetitions of her "joke."

Variation

Quoting your child's other interesting statements to other adults in front of your child is a good way of making her feel important and showing that you really listen to her.

Note

Many parents quote their children to other adults, but not always in front of the child, and the child is the one who has the most to gain from such an exchange.

DON'T YOU EVER TRY TO TICKLE A PICKLE

Purpose

To play the game of rhyming, which will facilitate the development of reading.

Game

In a singsong voice, emphasizing the italicized words, chant the following while acting out gestures you name:

Don't you ever try to *tickle* (tickle child) a *pickle* because a *pickle* will *tickle* (tickle child even longer here) you back.

And don't you every try to *blow* on a *toe* because a *toe* will *blow* you right back.

And don't you ever try to *sneeze* on *bees* because *bees* will *sneeze* on your back.

Don't you ever try to *squeeze* some *knees* because *knees* will *squeeze* you right back.

Don't you ever try to *rake* (make raking motion with your hand) a *snake* because a *snake* will *rake* you right back.

And don't you ever try to *spank Hank* because *Hank* will *spank* you right back.

And don't you ever try to *lick* a *stick* because a *stick* will *lick* you right back.

Don't you ever try to *pat* a *rat* because a *rat* will *pat* you right back.

(Whisper every once in a while) And don't you ever try to *rub Bub* because *Bub* will *rub* you right back.

Don't you ever try to *pinch* the *Grinch* because the *Grinch* will *pinch* you right back.

Don't you ever try to *scold* (shake your finger and look stern) a *cold* because a *cold* will *scold* you right back.

And don't you ever try to *growl* at an *owl* because an *owl* will *growl* at you back (say "Whooorrrrrrrrrrr").

And never ever try to *scowl* at a *fowl* because a *fowl* will *scowl* right back.

Don't you ever try to *bowl* at a *towel* because a *towel* will *bowl* you right back.

And don't you ever try to *zipper* (pretend to zip up your child's arm) a *flipper* because a *flipper* will *zipper* you back.

And don't you ever try to *blow* on *snow* because *snow* will *blow* on you back.

Don't you ever try to *kiss* a *tissue* because a *tissue* will *kiss* you right back.

Don't you ever try to *tackle* a *grackle* because a *grackle* will *tackle* you back.

Don't you ever try to *rock* a *sock* because a *sock* will *rock* you right back.

Don't you ever try to *bug* a *rug* because a *rug* will *bug* you right back.

Variations

1. Repeating just one sequence over and over has been known to get a lot of laughs from a two-year-old.

2. Make up your own gestures and rhymes and fit them into the general pattern given here.

3. My daughter came up with her own version of this game at the age of two and a half. She made up a series of nonsense words that rhymed and plugged them into the frame: "Don't you ever try to eye a sneye 'cause a sneye will eye you right back."

Note

This is a good game to play when your child has lost interest in whatever toys are around at the time, since you make yourself into the best of toys.

FRAMES

Purpose

Believe it or not, children at the tender age of two are capable of learning about parts of speech on a simple and important level. This game is designed to encourage that lesson.

Game

Just because a birthday is all over doesn't mean that you have to stop singing the birthday song with your child. In a singsong voice, begin to sing happy birthday to everything in sight: "Happy Birthday, Dear Cat! Happy Birthday, Dear Pretzel! Happy Birthday, Dear Petunia! Happy Birthday, Dear Little Red Riding Hood Book! Happy Birthday, Dear Ceiling!" There is no need to sing the whole song each time. The fun of the game comes when you take turns with your child substituting nouns into the "dear" slot. Make sure you encourage her to take a turn. See how imaginative you both can become with these substitutions. Actually sing the whole song for the wilder suggestions. Did you ever think you would find yourself singing happy birthday to a water pistol?

Although the list is endless, other especially workable noun frames include:

"That's a nice little truck. That's a nice little fan. That's a nice little hand. And that's a nice little potato."

"That's as big as a truck. That's as big as a dinosaur. That's as big as a watermelon. That's as big as a water tower. That's as big as a mountain. That's as big as _____."

"We could go to the store or we could go to the playground

or we could go to a big rock or we could go to Texas or we could go to the moon. Where else could we go?"

Variation

Shift to verb frames. Say something like, "I know a monkey who sings. And I know a monkey who dances. I know a monkey who whistles. And I know a monkey who prances. What kind of monkey do you know?"

Or: "This little finger is pointing. This little finger is hopping. This little finger is waving. This little finger is sleeping." Act out the actions you name, of course.

✳ 6 ✳

Preschool:
Three to Five Years

Perhaps the biggest development during this time may seem like a setback. Your preschooler will have already developed some endings for words. He probably says such things as "Daddy worked," as well as "Jimmy work," and "Two dogs," as well as "(One) Dog Bark." But in the next year or so, many more of these endings will appear. It is important to remember that your child will overapply a rule once he has learned it. Children are more systematic than our language is. They will say "Give me some more sugars" and "I comed home" or "I hi-ed the man" because they have learned that you use *s* when you mean more than one thing and *ed* when you talk about something you did yesterday. These "mistakes" actually show how much your child is thinking about language. He eventually will sort out these exceptions to the rules without too much comment on your part. You might just repeat what he says only using the correct form rather than telling him he has said something wrong.

Researchers have found that children who are corrected a lot talk less often than, and not as well as, children whose parents respond to what they are saying rather than how they are saying it. In this regard children resemble adults, I believe. Do you want to talk to someone who is continually correcting your pronunciation or grammar rather than listening to what you are saying?

Your preschool child will develop the ability to understand and produce complex sentences. Acting Out is a game that works with this ability.

Your child also will develop a number of skills that will result in reading. He will learn to discriminate letters and numbers and typically will recognize some "sight" words such as his name, "STOP," "EXIT," and "Dr. Seuss." Robot Talk and RITNG are games to develop these skills.

Children will make many errors in pronouncing words until they are eight or nine years old. The best thing to do about these speech errors at this age level is to provide the correct pronunciation for your child. Chants is a game that provides a technique for pronouncing new, difficult words.

You may find that your child begins to stutter sometime between the ages of two and five years. Stuttering is three to eight times more likely to happen with boys for some unknown reason. The question is, what should you do about stuttering? Again, the answer is DO NOTHING. THE WORST THING YOU CAN DO IS WORRY ABOUT YOUR CHILD'S STUTTERING AND LET HIM KNOW THAT YOU ARE WORRIED ABOUT IT.

First of all, we all stutter upon occasion, some of us more than others. You should be aware of the fact that the diagnosis of problem stuttering is highly unreliable, even among trained professionals. In other words, you may think your child is a stutterer, but professionals would not.

Second, over fifty percent of all stutterers recover by the time they reach puberty without any treatment at all. Eighty percent of all child stutterers recover by their late teens. If your child has not recovered by the time he is eighteen, I would recommend a behavior modification treatment program, since this type of program seems to have the most success.

There are many elaborate theories about why children stutter. A popular psychodynamic theory maintains that stuttering is an expression of anxiety stemming from a deep, unconscious conflict. There is no support for this theory. In fact, we still do not know what really causes stuttering. What we do know is that stuttering makes everyone anxious, including the stutterer, and anxiety makes all of us stutter more than we do when we are relaxed. In other words, once it starts, stuttering perpetuates itself to the extent that it creates anxiety in the speaker and his audience.

Of course, your child still will be working on vocabulary, though you may not realize it. The child of a friend of mine, who had been prepared carefully by her mother for the death scene in *E.T.*, went to the movie and continually asked "Is he dead yet?" Her mother feared that her strategy had backfired and her daughter had developed a preoccupation with death, but the little girl really only thought of death as a "special kind of sleep," as her mother had described it to her. Games like Marbles, Chants, Rhymes, and What Is a Shoe, Anyway? deal with various aspects of learning more about the meaning of words.

A number of people have noted that very young children are natural poets. For example, a twenty-month-old child may pretend to ride a box, calling it a horse even though he knows the correct name for it. A two-year-old may call paisley "worms." A child of three may say that he is "barefoot all over" in reference to the fact that he is naked. A four-year-old may refer to skywriting as "a scar in the sky" or a woman's nylon-clad legs as "chicken legs." Each child will produce his own unique metaphors.

Young children do not have nearly the number of words in their vocabularies that you have, and so they make extensive use of what words they do have, which results in a number of delightful, unwitting metaphors. But young children also unabashedly use pretend names for things whose proper names they know perfectly well, calling a piece of string "my tail" immediately after calling it "string."

In fact, I have observed some children playing metaphor games by themselves. A little girl not yet three was eating a slice of bologna. She asked her mother the name of it. Then she proceeded to eat it and play with it after each bite left it looking like another object. She called it, successively, "circle" and "moon of salami" several times before biting into it. Then she bit it and swung it and said "swing," bent it over and said "slide," took another large bite, made it glide along and said, "sailboat." Several bites later, she looked at it and said, "piggy," pointing to various parts of it, saying, "ears," "tail." She made a sailing motion and said, "sailboat sailing in the sea" several more times. After another bite, she said "flag," then another bite produced a "whale." Finally, she took another bite and said it was "like a lady. Teeth, nose, eyes, that's like a lady," pointing to appropriate parts. I was watching in the background, recording and taking down what she said. She was simply having fun by herself.

Your young child will tend to produce metaphors based on the similarity of shape between two things, as in the bologna example. As he grows older, your child also will use color and texture as a basis for metaphor. A few of his metaphors will not make much sense, but many will seem appealing and appropriate. For example, children have been known to call a dishwashing tool with strips of orange sponge attached to a plastic handle a wind-mill (three years), a tree with fall leaves (four years), and a palm tree (five years).

Metaphor Games 1 and 2 and Cloud Game capitalize on this natural ability to produce poetic language. They can and should be played through elementary school. Unfortunately, researchers have found that many children invent pretend names less fre-quently as they grow older, perhaps because they come to prefer literal language—using the "real" names for things—or perhaps because teachers explicitly discourage metaphors. Teachers may be so concerned to teach children the proper use of language that they inadvertently chase creative "mistakes" underground along with less creative ones. Whatever the case may be, you can have a lot of fun with your child creating metaphors, and it will en-courage his imagination.

David Dickinson and Catherine Snow have studied many children from the age of three years to see what kinds of ex-periences at home and in preschool predict the most successful development of language and reading. These researchers now have information on how the children are doing in kindergarten. First of all, as this book has emphasized, there are many contexts that support children's language and literacy development at home and at school. Children must have books read to them, as I have said repeatedly, but there are also completely oral language games that predict reading achievement in these children. Different strands of the complicated French braid of language are supported in different ways at different ages at home and in school. For example, the amount of time children spend engaging in pretend play with other children at school at the age of three predicts children's literacy development by kindergarten age. It may surprise some to learn that children who played fantasy games with their peers were ahead of other children who received more direct alphabet drill from their teachers.

What would Dickinson and Snow recommend you look for in your child's preschool experience, if you are interested in promoting his language and prereading skills? First, avoid the school where children of this age are drilled in the alphabet. Instead, look for the school or daycare center that provides the opportunity for many experiences in small groups of three or four children, where teachers read and discuss books or talk to children in a responsive manner, and embed discussions of the alphabet in ongoing activities of interest to the child (for example, figuring out which book belongs to him versus his friend by looking at the initials in the front). Look for teachers who encourage children to ask questions and make comments about books as they are read. Look for a preschool where there is a lot of animated talking by both teachers and children. Look for teachers who talk *with* rather than *at* or *down to* or *in front of* or *above* children.

What would Dickinson and Snow recommend you do with your child at home to promote language and literacy development during these preschool years? To begin with, children's vocabulary at the age of five years reflects the extent to which families had exchanged narratives or explained connections between events, objects, or concepts at dinnertime during the two preceding years—not at all an obvious connection. Furthermore, children's kindergarten performance on a standard test of their language and prereading skills, as well as their understanding of basic concepts, reflected the extent to which, earlier on, they had provided information to their mothers about what had happened to them in the past, as well as the extent to which their families exchanged narratives and discussed books while reading them. Exchanging narratives at dinner about what happened to family members also predicted children's ability to show that they understood a make-believe story read to them. In a nutshell, then, what parents can do to support their children's language and reading development is to play the kinds of games suggested in this book. Of particular importance in this regard are Tell a Story to Get a Story and Explanations.

In no small part because of different language experiences at home and school, individual differences in language development are marked although not new in kind. Cognitive and language development are so intertwined at this age that I will depart from my usual order of talking about emotions and then cognition to consider cognitive development first.

Your preschool child often will come up to you and say things like "He hit me hard on purpose and I hate Mrs. Beasley" without bothering to tell you who "he" is or how Mrs. Beasley entered the picture. Since you were not around at the time the child was hit, you may have the sense that your child is egocentric, that he feels the world revolves around him and everyone sees what he sees.

The great inventor of the study of cognitive development, Jean Piaget, argued that children were incapable of understanding that other people literally do not see things the same way as they do. Piaget placed a set of three "mountains" of various heights on a table, with a child on one side and a doll directly across the table from the child. He then asked the child what the doll "saw." Until the age of 7 to 8 years, the child invariably picked an (incorrect) arrangement of mountains, an arrangement identical to what he, the child, saw rather than the correct, reverse arrangement. Piaget argued that this sort of mistake was a sign of childhood egocentrism, and that egocentrism limited many childhood cognitive skills.

It is true that your child will often say "See this" about something that you cannot possibly see, since you are across the room at the time. But a number of researchers, myself included, have found that children at times are capable of showing that they know that others have perspectives on things that are not identical to their own. The key to showing a child's ability to understand another's point of view lies in making the task simple enough. For example, five-year-olds can tell you that Mommy would like to have a sweater rather than a doll for her birthday.

In other words, your child's vagueness in the Mrs. Beasley example has more to do with the fact that he still has a lot to work on in putting together sentences to make a good, coherent story. One of your child's biggest accomplishments during these preschool years is beginning to be able to tell a good narrative, one that can be understood even by people who are not present at the events being talked about. Games like I Don't See What You See and Tell a Story to Get a Story are aimed at developing a child's storytelling technique.

At other times, your preschooler will talk to himself, muttering things like, "Now color that red, now we take this off." This type of egocentric language is the way he is learning to plan his actions. Similarly, at other times such language is used to control his behavior. For example, one three-year-old girl was watching a children's play about a rabbit who was misbehaving himself. In the middle of the performance, apropos of nothing, she said, "I won't throw my shoe at that boy rabbit. No!" Since no one had suggested she do any such thing, it is obvious that she was strongly tempted to throw her shoe at the rabbit. She displayed self-control by verbalizing that command to herself.

Some parents are disturbed by this private, uncommunicative speech. They should not be. The brighter your child, the earlier he will use a lot of private speech, especially if he interacts well and frequently with playmates. In early elementary school, many children still mutter to themselves, and it seems as if this muttering is genuinely beneficial to their performance of difficult assignments. Private speech largely disappears by the age of nine. However, in my experience, even adults plan aloud in much the same way as children when they are pressed for time.

Related to the issue of egocentrism is the issue of how well, if at all, preschoolers understand causes and effects. Piaget and others have argued that children do not understand much at all about causality until they are about eight years old. It is true that if you ask your three-year-old child why it is cold outside, for example, he occasionally will give answers like my three-year-old daughter's: "Because there's snow on the ground." Once in a while he spontaneously may say something such as what my daughter said to me: "You know what the problem is? That your throat didn't have enough food to go in it. That's because you got sick." In both cases, the child reversed cause and effect.

However, Carole Peterson and I have found that younger children often perform poorly in tasks assessing their ability to reason because they do not understand what researchers are asking them to do or because what they are asked to do exceeds their memory limitations. Because is a game Carole Peterson and I invented that successfully improved the ability of four- and five-year-olds to understand sentences using "because" correctly. As far as their spontaneous speech goes, we found that children are no more likely to reverse cause and effect than are adults.

Preschool children are famous for their interminable causal questioning: "Why does the wind blow?" Parents who are interested in encouraging this intellectual initiative may find themselves continually running to an encyclopedia for answers to questions they have not thought about or studied for years. All very well and good, but the frustrating part of this is that children often are not satisfied by detailed explanations of the scientific causes of things. What preschoolers usually want in response to their questions is some notion of the consequences of something for them. The sun shines to make their garden grow or to let them play outside. A toy car has wheels so they can push it. The wind blows so they can fly kites. Try this sort of explanation next time you feel your patience waning in the face of seemingly endless whys.

I have also found it very amusing to turn the tables on young children. That is, ask your child a series of questions about why somebody got sick or why there is snow outside or why you got angry with them. You will find it very revealing, and your child probably will feel quite proud to be consulted in this way. Whenever I do this sort of thing, I am amazed continually not by how incompetent children are but by how much they do know, even at such a young age, about the world around them.

Another accomplishment during this period is that of classification. By the time he is four or five, your child will be very able to sort things out by colors or shapes or sizes. There are a number of toys that encourage such sorting. The game of Marbles is designed to help develop this ability.

One limitation to preschool thought is its black-or-white character. A preschool child will consider a person to be either old or young. A three-year-old may express strong distaste for a picture of her mother as a young child, or a four-year-old will think that her mother is lying when the mother says things like, "When I was little, I . . . " Similarly, things are either near or far. A preschooler will not understand that "the school is nearer than the grocery store but farther than Grandma's house." People are either big or little. You may find your four-year-old pressing the point of whether he is going to be big when he turns five. You repeatedly say, "Well, you'll be bigger than you are now, but not as big as me," which will fall on deaf ears and be met with a repetition of the question.

Throughout this preschool period your child will be working on his ability to get past this categorical thinking and arrange things in a serial order, from shortest to longest, from youngest to oldest, from lightest to darkest, etc. By seven or eight, he will be able to do this without error, although he will show some ability to order things before this time.

Preschool children are also easily swayed by the appearance of things, a limitation that It Looks Like a Cow but It's Really a Log is designed to help overcome. As children approach school age, they begin to master which visual changes signify material changes and which do not.

Your child's remarkable development in language and thought has a dramatic impact on his emotional development at this stage of his life. In this age range is the onset of what attachment theorists call the phase of goal-corrected partnership. In a close emotional relationship at any age, the two people involved share the mutual goal of wanting to spend a great deal of time together. The world interferes with this. Plans take them elsewhere, but they negotiate these separations. Your child is now capable of such negotiation. You really can ask him to wait for a minute until you stir the soup before you hug him. He has the language and the mental capacity to cope with such negotiations. As for longer separations, they still will be difficult. They remain so throughout life for any two people who love each other. But language is a bridge over such separations. You now can temper satisfactorily the difficulty of long separations by phone conversations with your child.

You are not the only emotional force in your child's life now. Your preschooler happily will leave you to spend a lot of time playing with other children. It is inevitable that he will get into fights. All children hit and kick from time to time. You should understand that this is normal. However, you should also make it plain to your child that fighting is unacceptable behavior. Some parents I have known actually encourage their children, especially their sons, to be aggressive under the misguided notion that to be aggressive is to be a leader. This is unfortunate for all concerned, their child's victims and their child. Overwhelming evidence suggests that to be aggressive in nursery school and kindergarten (and thereafter) is to be perceived as a bully. Children almost universally reject bullies. Children are not crazy. Who likes to be hit and kicked?

Related to physical aggression is verbal aggression, insulting and rejecting others, swearing, criticizing, etc. Again, you must understand it both as normal and as unacceptable. The game of Hurtful Words is one way of dealing with this verbal aggression.

Preschool children display considerable individual differences in virtually every facet of language development. Some children are almost ready to read by age four, some children do not show much reading readiness until age six or so. Some children are lively storytellers, some are reticent. Some children enunciate quite distinctly, others talk in a somewhat mushy way. Some swear like the proverbial troopers, others almost never say anything nasty to anyone. All this variation is well within the normal range.

But perhaps even more striking than these individual differences are the gender differences that emerge during this time. Now that your child is tuned into the fact that the world divides into boys and girls, he may exaggerate the differences between the two even if you try to downplay these differences. I know quite a number of anecdotes about little boys who see their fathers cook at home, yet return from nursery school to announce that "boys don't cook." Or a little girl who knows that her mother is a doctor who comes home and argues that "only boys can be doctors, girls have to be nurses." Girls may insist on wearing dresses every day even though their mothers wear pants all the time. These exaggerated gender differences show up in language. Generally speaking, preschool boys are fonder than girls of loud sound effects (crashes and shootings and the like), insults, and other verbal aggression, such as obscenities.

It is quite a lot of fun to talk to preschool children. Many of the games in this section are really just for fun, although they may have other beneficial side effects. Rhymes, Tell a Story to Get a Story, RITNG, and the Metaphor Games are the most important to your child's general development and will contribute to his readiness for reading. Also, your preschool child still will enjoy most of the language games I have described so far in this book.

TELL A STORY TO GET A STORY

Purpose

To find out what has happened to your child when you have been apart, to see how he feels about what has happened, and to work on his storytelling skills.

Game

Engage your child in a task, such as drawing a picture, in order to minimize his self-consciousness about talking. While he is drawing, tell him about something that the picture or some other object reminds you of. Telling a story about yourself works better than simply asking questions to get children of this age to talk to you. The trick is to tell stories about things that happened to you that were exciting or otherwise important and that also are likely to have happened to your child. For example, you might say something like this:

> When I was your age, I once ripped my shirt when we were playing outside. We were sliding down the sliding board, and my shirt caught on the slide going down, and it ripped. When I got off the slide, everybody laughed at me and I was embarrassed. I wore my jacket for the rest of the day. Did anything like that ever happen to you?

> *Or:* When I was in first grade, I used to do all right, but there were a lot of kids who did better than me. But one day we were supposed to draw pictures of our house. And I drew the best picture, so I got to draw the outline for the picture of our school that the class worked on together. That was fun, being the best in the class at something.

> *Or:* I used to be such a good girl in school. Except for one time when I was talking to my boyfriend and he made a joke. We weren't even supposed to be talking, but I didn't care. He was a really nice boy. Anyway, he told me a joke about frogs and I started laughing so hard I couldn't stop. My face got red, and the teacher yelled at me in front of the whole class.

There are hundreds of things to talk about. If you sense that something happened to upset your child and you want to get him to talk about it, try to come up with something close to what you think probably happened rather than just asking him outright. This lets the child know that it is okay to be yelled at by the teacher or to be unpopular with his peers on occasion or to be embarrassed or forgetful or what have you. It also will allow your child to get to know you better. Similarly, your child's responding narrative will tell you not only exactly what happened but also how he feels about it (see Note).

By the way, do not preface your narratives by saying, "I am going to tell you a story now." Children associate the word "story" with something that is made up and will take off on another language game, Once Upon a Time, described on pages 100–101.

Follow up your own narratives with such prompting questions as, "Did anything like that ever happen to you? Tell me about it." You will need to use more specific questions for younger children. For example, say you have just told your three-year-old a story about being beaten up by a bully when you were in kindergarten. If you ask, "Has anything like that ever happened to you?" and get no response, try, "Well, did you ever get yelled at by other kids?" or "Did you ever get left out of a game?" Older children will make greater leaps, sometimes needing only one narrative from you to trigger a dozen from them, but you have to hit the specific experience of three- or four-year-olds pretty much on the head.

Remember, though, you want to avoid turning this into an interrogation. So if you ask several questions and get no response, drop the topic and move on to a new one. I view this narrative game as a fishing expedition. You will get some nibbles, some short responses, but it takes a lot of casts to get your child to really bite and come up with a truly good narrative. It is well worth the effort.

Once your child is underway, repeat part of what he has just said from time to time in order to let him know you are listening closely. Ask questions after he is finished about parts of his narrative that were not clear.

Variations

1. Have a large group of people take turns telling stories on a theme. For example, take turns telling about the scariest or the saddest or the funniest or the most embarrassing thing that ever happened to you. I have played this version of this game with adults as well as with children and have had a good time.

2. Create a setting to go with your theme. For example, you might go down to the cellar on Halloween, light a single candle, and take turns telling about the scariest thing that ever happened to you. Of course, make sure that your children are old enough not to be too scared by this. Or you might put on clown outfits or other silly disguises and tell about the funniest thing that ever happened to you. Or you might celebrate Christmas afternoon by telling about the most special thing that ever happened to you. A hot summer's afternoon would be a great time to sip cold drinks, put ice bags on yourselves, and tell each other about the time you were the coldest you have ever been.

3. Do the same thing as in Variation 2, but make up stories instead of telling about real things that happened to you. Make up the scariest story you can on Halloween. If your family is not spooked easily, you even could take a trip to a scary setting—an old, abandoned house or barn, for example, and make up a story about what happened there.

Note

Adults almost automatically try to get children to talk by asking them questions, such as, "What did you do in school today?" After all, questions have worked very well in getting children to respond ever since they were two. Unfortunately, preschool children almost as automatically reply, "Worked" or "Played" or some other monosyllable. Parents come back with a more specific question, "Did you have fun?" Children reply, "Yes." End of interrogation. No narrative. But this game provides a good alternative to frustrating interrogation.

Of course, if you want to know what your child thinks about things, eventually you will have to resist the temptation to say, "Oh, that must have been scary," or "I bet you were really upset." With a very young child, you well might need to provide such opportunities to learn the names of appropriate emotions. But as your child grows up, do less of the work for him. He will tell you how he felt, and his feelings may surprise you.

This technique works well at getting children to talk about unpleasant events, such as deaths of pets or relatives or car accidents they unfortunately may have witnessed. Again, if you want to know what your child thinks about a disturbing event, tell him a story about something similar that happened to you—the time your grandfather died or the time your cat ran away or the time you saw a motorcycle accident. Encourage your child to talk about what happened in this indirect way rather than simply asking him outright what he thinks about what happened. Children will be more likely to talk about the upsetting experience in response to hearing about a similar experience, although they typically express less emotion about a relative or pet who has died than they do about one who is still living. Perhaps it is too painful to them to think about feelings they still have for the dead.

Note also that if you have been with your child during the disturbing event in question, you may have to have another adult elicit your child's version of the experience. Children tell more of an event to a fresh audience than to someone who has experienced the event with them.

EXPLANATIONS

Purpose

To give your child an understanding of the ways people and things and language works, and to foster your child's language and literacy skills.

Game

During conversations over meals or on rides or whenever they occur, point out connections between events or objects or concepts. Explain your feelings, commands, questions, and actions to your child. Tell her why you do what you do, as the following mother does:

> MOTHER: What do we do with your fingernails?
> CHILD: Cut them!
> MOTHER: Yes, why do we cut them?
> CHILD: I scratch Billy.
> MOTHER: Do you remember that?
> CHILD: Yeah.

Explain physical events such as why seeds grow. Explain why accidents occur. Explain what words mean. Explain what objects are like. Explain how you do things like cooking omelets or going skating. Explain how you know the things you do. Explain the consequences of misbehavior, such as, "If you cross the road without looking, a car might hurt you very badly."

Variation

As always, the best variation is to turn the tables and ask your child to explain something. Ask her to explain why she did something before you discipline her. Occasionally she may persuade you that her actions were justified. Ask her to show you how to work complicated toys she may have mastered before you have. Ask her to explain things to her younger brother. By encouraging her to explain simple procedures, you will be preparing her for the kind of explanatory talk that is valued in schools.

Note

Parents who explain the way the world works to their children are doing many very good things. They are helping their children understand that other people have feelings, plans, and intentions that may affect the children and that children need to come to understand in order to get along with other people. In providing explanations of physical events, such parents provide science lessons on a daily basis to their children. Recently, as I pointed out in the introduction to this section, the provision of such explanations predicts children's development of a substantial vocabulary, among other prereading skills. Finally, parents who habitually reason with their children have been found many times to have children who achieve more academically and have higher self-esteem, compared to children whose parents continually resort to the old dictation, "Do this because I tell you to."

Work by Carole Peterson and myself, Diane Beals, and Morag Donaldson has brought to our attention the variety of explanations some parents offer their children on a daily basis. We have also found cases, unfortunately, of parents who seldom provide such explanations. Explanations take time, and children have a way of requesting them when you are in a less than talkative mood, such as when you are putting your child to bed or trying to get her to do something. However, there are few things more important to your child's social, cognitive, and linguistic skills. Knowing that explanations are so important might help in those moments of extreme exasperation when your child asks for the hundredth time why she has to brush her teeth.

BIG GIRLS DON'T CRY

Purpose

To make a game out of disciplinary comments while rehearsing them.

Game

You have told your daughter a thousand times to put her pajamas in the hamper in the morning, to brush her teeth before she goes to bed, to say "Please" and "Thank you" and "Excuse me." You have told her countless times not to hit people or kick them or bite them or call them names. You can either fear that you are losing your mind and turning into a tape recorder, or you can turn these disciplinary refrains into a game.

The game goes like this: You name one thing that big girls do (Big girls feed the cat) or don't do (Big girls don't hit their baby brothers), and then your child names another thing that they do or don't do. Go back and forth. The first person who draws a blank gets tickled.

Variation

Try the same thing using other contrasts. For example, you might try "Babies cry" or "Forgetful girls don't make their bed" or "Barbarians put their feet on the coffee table." Again, take turns naming things that babies or forgetful girls or barbarians do. Some children will become quite inventive here.

Note

You will want to avoid talking repeatedly about "bad" boys or "bad" girls because too much such labeling can be psychologically damaging to your child, resulting either in a self-fulfilling prophecy or a poor self-concept or both. You also will want to avoid passing sexism to your children by telling your sons such things as, "Boys don't cry; only girls cry."

DREAM REPORT

Purpose

To find out what your child is thinking about at night, and to teach him how to talk about dreams.

Game

Every morning, just after he wakes up, ask your child what he is thinking about. Ask him how he feels. Talk about the fact that dreams are not about things that really happened, especially if he tells you that he had a scary dream. Try to trace his scary dreams to television shows, misunderstood comments, and so forth, and explain that his dream was something that *happened inside his head* because he was thinking about a television show, for example. My three-year-old daughter came up with a perfect solution to having a scary dream: she just "shaked the dream out of (her) head."

Variation

Tell your child what you dreamed about, and what you think it meant.

Note

Your preschool child is in the process of sorting through what things are "real" and what things are "pretend" and what things are something in between, like dreams, which "happen in your head." You will need to talk to your child a lot to help him sort through all this. If you want another conversation starter along these lines, ask your four-year-old whether Cookie Monster is real or pretend. My three-year-old daughter insisted that he was real for a long time, while I insisted he was pretend. We resolved the controversy finally by saying he was a "real muppet."

Even after your preschool child learns that dreams are not things that "really happened," he may believe that you can "see" his dreams. Talk with him about the fact that you cannot see his dreams, nor can he see your dreams. It will take a while before your child really understands that his vivid nightly experience is really a collection of his own private thoughts.

MARBLES

Purpose

To teach your child the technical descriptions for things.

Props

To begin with, you need a shape-sorter toy, such as Fisher-Price's First Blocks, and a puppet of some sort. As your child masters the description of one set of toys, move on to another set. Marbles are so varied that they make an inexpensive but rich sort of prop for this game.

Game

The game consists of pointing out a few terms at a time and having the puppet ask for one or another type of object. First work on colors, then shapes (square or circular blocks), numbers, and patterns (cat's eye or swirly or solid type of marble). For example, begin your first session of Marbles with the Fisher-Price blocks by saying, "This is a *blue* block, and this is another blue block, and this is another blue block. And this is a *red* block. This is another red block, and this is another red block. Now Froggie, what kind of block do you want?" Froggie says, "Give me a blue one. I want a blue one right now, please. No, that's a red one. Could I have a blue one, please? Thank you."

Eventually, after outgrowing the blocks, Froggie plays with marbles and says such things as, "I want three green swirlies and two white solids in this basket right here, please. Thank you."

Variation

Fair Trade: Give your child the set of marbles, your spouse the set of blocks, and yourself a set of play beads or coins or some other set of things you want to teach your child to describe. You trade her three sets of violet beads for two green cat's eyes. Note that this variation works only for more advanced Marble players.

Note

This is so obviously an instructional game that it surprises me how much fun it is for even very young children. One two-year-old I know likes to play Marbles for almost an hour at a time. Her parents tire of the game long before she does and are usually the ones to break it off.

I DON'T SEE WHAT YOU SEE

Purpose

The general purpose of the game is to encourage your child to give clear, complete descriptions and requests. The specific goal of the game is for your child to succeed at telling you what to do with a set of objects that are hidden from your view.

Props

Blank screen of some sort (uninteresting, nondistracting hard-cover book or manila folder or tablet), two dump trucks and two identical sets of pictures or plastic animals for three-year-olds (1), two identical sets of marbles or colored blocks for older children (2). Variation 3 calls for a felt board.

Game

Put one set of materials on each side of the screen. Seat yourself on the opposite side of the screen from your child. Ask your child to choose an object, put it in his dump truck, and tell you which object it is so that you can put the same object in your dump truck. When he has told you what to put in the truck and you have done so, both of you should roll your trucks out from behind the screen and see if you have the same objects in them.

Keep your instructions short and simple: "You have a set of blocks, and I have a set of the same kinds of blocks. I am going to put this folder between us so that I can't see what you are doing. I want you to put one block in your dump truck and describe it to me so I can put the same kind of block in my dump truck." Be sure to dramatize the moment of truth: "Ready, set, go! Up with the screen!"

Deliberately make mistakes if your child does not tell you clearly or specifically enough and explain why you made the mistake: "Oops, I have the blue dog and you have the green one. You will have to tell me which color you want the next time." Make these "mistakes" by delaying the emergence of your dump truck until you surreptitiously peek at his choice. Put the wrong one in and then roll it out. But do not let the game disintegrate into a series of corrections. If one set of materials proves too hard, try a simpler set (see Note). If your child still does not tune into the game, try the Marbles game instead. Above all, enjoy yourselves.

Variations

1. Switch roles; tell your child what to put in his dump truck. Be deliberately vague sometimes and encourage your child to correct you in order to improve his ability to get the information he needs from people. For example, if there are two different pigs, one blue and one pink, just tell your child to "put the pig in the dump truck." No matter which pig he puts in the truck, say you wanted the other one. Encourage him to protest that you were not clear enough about what you wanted. Point out your own (deliberate) shortcomings if your child does not do so.

2. Use different specific goals. Instead of asking your child to put something in a dump truck, ask him to make a tower or some other construction out of colored blocks. Have him tell you how to make the same kind of tower. Make sure that your child gives you directions as he goes along, rather than his waiting until he has

finished. Dramatize the moment of truth by saying, "And now, ladies and gentlemen, we will see how well we have done." Give drum roll, etc. Again, explain how you made mistakes.

3. Older children can be given a set of pictures of forms for a felt board. Have your child tell you what design to make and how to make it.

Note

In the introduction to this section, we discussed Piaget's ideas that young children are egocentric. Piaget described egocentrism as an immature cognitive state that simply would disappear as the child grew older. He did not believe that you could train a child to be less egocentric. But other researchers have discovered that you *can* train a child to seem less egocentric. Their training task is the basis of this game, which is fun for children four to eight years old. Even three-year-olds will enjoy playing a simplified version of the game. Attention spans vary, depending upon age and the individual child. As a rule, this game will hold a four- or five-year-old child's attention for ten to fifteen minutes.

A prerequisite for playing this game is the knowledge of specific technical terms (colors, shapes, patterns, forms, etc.), which is developed in the Marbles Game, a game you should continue to play with new forms. It is a good idea to use recognizable objects such as pictures or animals with three-year-olds, since they generally do not yet know all their color names. Four-year-olds tend to know color but not shape names, and are likely to resort to metaphor ("bulldozer wheel" was one child's way of referring to a long, thick yellow stick), so a set of colored identical shapes works for them, even encouraging a Metaphor Game. Five-year-olds generally know some shape names. Blocks of different colors and shapes make the best choice of material for children over three because they can be used in other types of games.

Most children will insist on switching roles (1), with you telling them how to make or do something. This variation allows you to see how successful you are at communicating with your child. This is also a good way of showing your child how the game is played, if he does not understand from your general instructions. Variation 1 also involves occasional deliberate vagueness on your part, which turns out to be very beneficial for your child. Children get a lot of inadequate (egocentric) messages from adults. Unless they learn to detect and comment on such inadequate instructions, they may blame themselves or be blamed by the adult culprits for the resulting errors.

This game sparks other games along the way. I already have mentioned how children will begin to play a Metaphor Game in their descriptions. They also will get involved in the conceptual game of building cars or dinosaurs or houses from abstract shapes. Sometimes they will tell you that they are building an airplane, for example. Other times, they even may spontaneously insist at the end of the session that you guess what they were trying to make.

JESSOSAURUS

Purpose

To teach children, while teasing them, that words are made up of syllables.

Props

A book about dinosaurs.

Game

After reading all the names of dinosaurs, substitute your child's name as follows: "If this is a stegosaurus, you must be a Jessosaurus."

"You are a Jessosaurus Rex."

"This is an iguanodon and you are a Jessodon."

"That one is diplodocus and you are Jessodocus."
"If this is triceratops, you must be Jessatops."

Variation

Try the same thing for other animals or birds. For example, if you enjoy bird watching and have a book on birds available, name some of the many different kinds of ducks or sparrows and substitute your child's name for the species' name: Jessa duck or Jessa sparrow.

HURTFUL WORDS

Purpose

To encourage creative teasing and the enjoyment of bantering, and to instruct your child in what is teasing versus what is hurtful talk.

Props

For the variation of this game proposed here, you will need some old lipstick, fake mustaches, a wig or two, and as many hats as you can find.

Game

When your child calls you a name, even a bad one, call her something that is not bad but usually not used in reference to people. For example, if she calls you "chicken legs," call her "chicken nose." If she calls you a noodle, call her a watermelon. If she calls you a tum-tee, call her a tum-tah. But if she calls you something that is actually nasty, like "poopiehead," stop the game by saying something like, "Oh, oh, you have gone too far. Don't be fresh. That's not a nice word. I say you are a giraffe." A very important rule of this game is that you can never repeat anything you said before, a rule that encourages creativity and discourages obscenity. I have found it necessary to repeat the rule frequently when a child repeatedly says, "poopiehead," for example.

Variation

Put on different combinations of hats, makeup, mustaches, and wigs between turns and have your child make up a name to call you in each disguise.

Note

When children have passed through the vocabulary explosion, use complicated four-, five-, and six-word sentences, and in general know as much language as the average three-year-old does, it is easy to lose sight of the fact that they are still in the process of learning language. Simply pronouncing a word correctly and using it in a somewhat appropriate way does not mean that a child knows fully what the word means. Children learn a lot about language in the act of producing it and seeing what effect it has. In the case of hurtful words, for instance, children seldom will know the full meaning of the words when they start to use them. Typically, they simply will have seen an older child get a rise out of someone with a word that they instantly commit to memory. Parents are placed in the curious position of having to teach their children a lot about the meaning of hurtful words even as they are instructing their children not to say such things because "it hurts people's feelings" or "good boys don't say things like that."

With naughty words like "caca," often produced very early on either as a lucky-guess random babble or as an imitation of other children, some parents use the strategy of ignoring their child, according to the theory that ignoring a behavior will make it drop out of a child's repertoire. But since the child's other language is, I hope, seldom ignored, the child is bound to notice that this word has a strange effect. Then, too, strangers will be likely to break the code of silence and react with a "naughty girl" or a laugh or some other instructive reaction. What is more, sooner or later you will be unwilling to chance your child's saying "caca" or "I hate you" to his grandparents, who have flown in from quite a distance to see their adorable grandchild, and so you will have to give up the strategy of ignoring such remarks and tell your child that he should not say them.

Since it is always a good strategy to tell your child why he should not do something, and since the "why" in this case is what the word means, you must be prepared to say something about what the word means. It will require a little creativity to come up with a child's version of some obscenities. I would not recommend lying to your child about the meaning of such words. By the age of four, most children these days have learned a lot about anatomy from other children, doctors, and parents, and other children will perhaps include some distortions along the way, if you do not step into the breach.

So far, this does not sound like much of a game, I admit. But name-calling can be turned into one. I particularly enjoy including this as a bona fide language game because I think most parents miss the language learning part of it. That they miss this aspect is testimony to the truly enormous power of language. Parents are so shocked to be called a "chicken" or a "poopiehead" that they will miss the fact that their child also refers to them with nonsense constructions like "pooky-pie." Your child is trying out a variety of ways of referring to you. Your child also at times may call you by your first name. Using a number of different words for the same thing shows that a child is tuning in to language. Having one way of referring to something is utilitarian; having more than one way of referring to something is not necessary but, instead, shows the kind of enjoyment of language for its own sake that eventually is the impulse for poetry. Using a number of different words for the same thing also will produce somewhat different reactions from listeners and will therefore result in more complete understanding of the subtle differences in the meanings of words.

This game encourages creativity and the enjoyment of bantering—a key component of assertiveness—at the same time that it instructs the child in words that are not fun but only hurtful. I find it a much better solution to a very natural impulse than simply saying, "We don't call people names," or "Name-calling is bad." Name-calling can be good fun—for adults, too.

VOICES

Purpose

To draw your child's attention to the existence of different registers, or different manners of speaking.

Props

Several puppets, one for each voice you want to use. See Corky for hints about homemade puppets.

Game

This game is really a puppet show, but the focus is not on telling a great story but on developing characters. To begin with, you might have the following conversations on different occasions:

1. A rude puppet named Boris talking to a polite puppet named Polly about playing with toys: "Give me those toys right now. I want them. They are mine," yells Boris. "I will be glad to share these toys with you, but won't you please say 'please' first?" says Polly in a quiet, polite way. "No, No, No!" roars Boris. And the conversation continues in this vein.

2. A whiny puppet named Brat talking to his dad about wanting some candy.

3. A stranger puppet named New Kid talking to two puppets named Alice and Emily, who are friends with each other. Alice might start off the conversation by saying, "Hi, New Kid. How are you? Would you like to play with this toy for a while?"

4. A doctor puppet named Dr. Nice talking to his patient, Belinda, about getting a shot. "I'm going to give you a shot now, Belinda, but it will feel just like a mosquito bite."

5. A dentist puppet named Dr. Smiles talking to her patient, Tommy Tooth (who tries to smile at everyone despite the fact that he has a cavity that makes his "head" hurt).

6. A big girl or big boy puppet talking to a baby puppet, explaining to the baby how to use a toy or how to dress himself or how to go to the grocery store.

Keep special puppets special by talking in a certain way only when you are playing this game. Repeat each routine frequently.

Variation

One natural variation is to have your child play one of the characters in the scene, whichever one he wants to play. In fact he probably will suggest this himself.

Note

Recent researchers have found many preschool children to be quite good at changing their style of speech depending on the character they play, but that such sensitivity increases with age and practice. This game is designed to encourage the practice of being polite or friendly or brave or helpful by dramatizing and rehearsing the differences between these positive styles of speaking and their negative counterparts.

BECAUSE

Purpose

To see how well your child understands the word "because" and to improve his comprehension.

Props

A clown puppet, girl and boy dolls, and a pen with a cap on it.

Game

Tell your child that the clown puppet, Gonzo, is a silly clown and that you and your child are going to try to teach him how to talk right. Say, "First, I'm going to play teacher, and then you're going to play teacher, okay? You're going to be just like (name of child's nursery school teacher). We have these two dolls here, and we're going to pretend that things happen to them, and then we're going to teach Gonzo how to talk about those things."

Scene 1: "Pretend that this mother doll is peeling some potatoes with a sharp knife, when all of a sudden, oops! She slips and cuts herself with the knife. Oh, look at that pretend blood. Now let's ask Gonzo what happened. Gonzo, what happened?"

In a Gonzo voice, reply: "She cut herself because she was bleeding."

In your own voice, shake your fingers at the puppet and say: "No, Gonzo, you silly clown. That's not right. You're supposed to say, 'She was bleeding because she cut herself.'"

In a Gonzo voice, say: "Well, can I say, 'She cut herself because the knife was sharp?'"

In your own voice: "That's right, Gonzo. That's the way to talk."

Scene 2: "Now let's pretend this girl doll is Molly and this boy doll is Billy. Molly and Billy are fighting, and all of a sudden Molly hits Billy, and Billy starts to cry. Billy goes, 'Boo hoo hoo.' How would you talk about that, Gonzo?"

In a Gonzo voice, say: "Molly hit Billy because he cried."

In your own voice: "No, no, Gonzo, that's not right, you silly clown. You're supposed to say, 'Billy cried because Molly hit him.' That's the right way to say it."

Gonzo: "Billy cried because Molly hit him."

You: "That's right. You did it right that time."

Scene 3: This time, you're going to play teacher. You tell Gonzo when he is saying things right and when he is being silly, okay? Now let's pretend that Billy has a glass of water, when all of a sudden he trips and whoosh, he spills the water."

In a Gonzo voice, say: "Billy tripped because he spilled the water."

If your child scolds Gonzo, praise him. If your child doesn't say anything, say, "Tell Gonzo what he should say." If your child says something irrelevant, say, "Gonzo is trying to say something about why things happen. Remember, he said, 'Billy tripped because he spilled the water.' How would you say that right?" If your child says that Gonzo was right, say, "What about if Gonzo said, 'The water spilled because Billy tripped?' That would be a better way of saying it, wouldn't it? I think that's what Gonzo really was trying to say."

Scene 4: "It is still your turn to be teacher. Let's pretend that this girl doll is Billy's mom. Billy is in a good mood and he wants to watch cartoons. He asks his mother if he is allowed to watch cartoons on TV, and his mother says, 'No, you can't.' Now Billy is really mad." (Make doll jump up and down madly and make a mad, pouty face like Billy would make.)

In a Gonzo voice say, "Billy is mad because he can't watch TV."

In your own voice say, "Is that the right way to talk?"

If your child correctly praises Gonzo, praise your child. If your child scolds Gonzo, say, "Now wait a minute. That one's right, isn't it? It is right to say, 'Billy is mad because he can't watch TV,' isn't it? Gonzo was trying so hard, and he said it just right, and now you've hurt his feelings."

Scene 5: "You are still Gonzo's teacher. Let's pretend that Billy got a brand new laser gun for Christmas. Pretend this (pen) is his laser gun. One day, Billy puts his laser gun down on a chair while he goes to the bathroom. And when he comes back he forgets it is there and sits on it, and oops! It breaks!" (Take off pen top to show that it breaks.)

Gonzo: "Billy sat on his laser because he broke it." (Repeat reactions to child's comment in Scene 3.)

If your child still is not understanding the game, give hints in a whispered voice "behind Gonzo's back." Make up other scenes, alternating whether Gonzo says something right or wrong. Preschool children love this game even when they do not understand it, and will take off into puppet play, another language game.

Variation

When your child has become good at this game, you may want to dispense with enacting the scenes and just give him a few sentences from Gonzo to judge as correct or incorrect. You can make up your own, but here are some for starters.

The man sat on his glasses because he broke them. (Silly)

She had to stay home from school today because she was sick. (Right)

The road had a long hill because the bus was going very fast. (S)

The window broke into pieces because the boy threw a ball at it. (R)

The bridge was broken because they couldn't drive the car over the bridge. (S)

We thought it would rain because the sky was very cloudy. (R)

The police put the man in jail because the man stole some money. (R)

The boy could fly the kite very high because the wind was blowing. (R)

He was feeling hungry because he ate all the chocolate cake. (S)

The shop was on fire because someone called the fire department. (S)

The girl kicked the boy because she was very angry at him. (R)

The boy fell off his new bicycle because he scraped his knee. (S)

We wanted to go skating tonight because the river was frozen over. (R)

The hat was under the chair because the little girl could not find it. (S)

The chair got very wet because the glass of water fell on it. (R)

The knife was very sharp because the little boy cut his finger. (S)

WHAT IS A SHOE, ANYWAY?

Purpose

To give your child practice in defining words in a simple way.

Props

A weird-looking puppet.

Game

Introduce the puppet as Marcia the Martian, who talks in a weird voice. Have Marcia go around the room asking what things are. Make it clear that although you know what the things are, Marcia does not. "What's this? A shoe, you say. What *is* a shoe anyway?" Your child will typically come up with a definition in terms of the use something has for him. "A shoe is for putting your foot in." Try: father, mother, ball, cup, dog, bed, coat, star, sun, bubble, soap, etc.

Variation

If your child is not interested immediately in this game, try reading Ruth Krauss's *A Hole Is to Dig: A First Book of First Definitions* (Harper & Row) as a warm-up to the game above.

CHANTS

Purpose

To give your child an enjoyable method pronouncing long, difficult words, to encourage him to repeat these words and commit them to memory, and to give him an appreciation for the musical rhythm of language.

Props

A dictionary is helpful if you yourself are unsure of the correct pronunciation of a word.

Game

Take a word that is difficult for your child to pronounce and begin to chant it over and over again, alternately raising, then lowering your voice. Exaggerate stress in the word and use a nearby table as a bongo drum, beating it slowly, in time with your chant. Have your child do the same thing. Be sure to define the word for your child. Although this game is primarily useful when your child comes across a word in a book or in conversation that trips up his tongue, the game is also fun to play for its own sake. The following words are good for starters. Note that stressed syllables are printed in capital letters, with the italicized syllable having the primary accent.

parasaurolophus (PAR-a-SAW-roh-*LOH*-fus)
styracosaurus (STY-*RAK*-oh-SAWR-us)

ankylosaurus (*AN*-kyl-oh-SAWR-us)
pronunciation (PRO-NUN-see-*AY*-shun)
pediatrician (PEE-DEE-uh-*TRI*-shun)
xylophone (ZIE-lo-phone)
garbanzo beans (gar-BON-zo BEANS)
Louisiana (LOO-eez-ee-*AN*-uh)
Mississippi (MISS-i-*SIP*-ee)
encyclopedia (EN-CYC-lo-*PEE*-DEE-uh)
particularly (par-*TIC*-u-LAR-lee)
ravioli (RAH-vee-*OH*-lee)
radiator (*RAY*-dee-AY-tor)

Variation

Rounds: Once your child has chanted a word to mastery, you can turn the chant into a sort of musical composition. To do this you need several people. Have your child begin by beating the rhythm of a word on a table, with special stress on the beat of the most accented syllable, and chanting the word over and over, and then have other members of the group chime in one at a time, speaking and beating the table also. Each person should start when the primary accented syllable is spoken by the person before them in line. This may take some practice at first, but it can become quite mesmerizing.

Note

Parents may be somewhat surprised to see me recommending that young children tackle the pronunciation of such long and complicated words. But I devised this game because, during the preschool years, many children develop a fascination with dinosaurs that I believe involves a fascination with pronouncing their long and complicated names as much as it does with their huge size and strange appearance. Once again I will repeat: normal children vary considerably in their ability and inclination to use language. If you find that even with this game a child finds some word too difficult, you should of course abandon the effort to teach it to him and talk about something else. But do not underestimate your child by not even attempting difficult words. This method of mastering the pronunciation of difficult words is more important than the specific words pronounced. I still find it useful myself occasionally.

RHYMES

Purpose

To teach your child about the sounds of words, an exercise that will help prepare your child for reading.

Game

Take any word and name another word that rhymes with it. Then have your child take a turn naming another rhyming word. For example, you say, "Night rhymes with light. What's another word that rhymes with night?" "Fight? Good. And I will say bite." Other good candidates for rhyming are can, nut, hot, mice, bear, star, bun. The first person who cannot come up with a rhyme gets tickled.

Variations

1. Go through the alphabet, taking turns with your child putting every letter in front of some combination such as *orn*: acorn, born, corn, (a)dorn, foreign (pronounced as forn), gorn (that doesn't make sense, does it?), horn, (ad)journ, Koran, (for)lorn, morn, norn (that doesn't make any sense either), pour in (slurred), quaran(tine), roar in, soar in, torn, vorn (I have never heard of a vorn), worn, xorn (really doesn't make sense), your'n (colloquial for "yours"), zorn (What could a zorn look like?). Or *old*: bold, cold, doled, fold, gold, hold, Joeled (if you know a Joel and think

of his characteristic actions: "Oh no, I've been Joeled," referring to being given a wet kiss perhaps), knolled (made a hill), lolled, mold, noeled (celebrated Christmas), polled, quarreled (in a Boston accent, dropping the r's), rolled, sold, told, voled (bitten by a vole, which is a small rodent), wold (What could that be?), extolled (close but no cigar), ye olde, zold (Would a zold be old?).

The combination *at* works very well, too. Point out combinations that are not words and, while you are at it, make up pretend definitions or characters, some of which will sound a lot like Dr. Seuss characters.

2. Have your child do all the rhyming, once he gets the hang of it. See how many words he can rhyme.

3. Give your child word puzzles involving rhyming. For example, say, "What starts with *V* and rhymes with culture?" "Right, vulture."

Note

Although most parents engage in some form of rhyming play with their children, they may not realize how important it is. A number of studies find that a five-year-old's ability to recognize and produce rhymes is highly related to his reading ability. Rhyming is not just a frill. It's a skill.

ADIOS

Purpose

To acquaint your child with foreign languages.

Props

For Variation 2, you need a sign language dictionary. These are becoming widely available. There is even a *Sesame Street* sign language dictionary to be found in most bookstores.

Game

Introduce your child to a foreign word for one of the English words given here each time you use it. Eventually, the Adios game is played by taking turns saying good-bye or hello or whatever in a different language. You say, "Adios," your child says, "Au revoir." You say, "Sayonara," your child says, "Auf Wiedersehen," and so forth, back and forth. For parents who are not bilingual, here are a few foreign words to begin with, with phonetic pronunciations of the ones most unlike English in parentheses beneath them:

English	Hello	Good-bye	Good night	Yes	Thanks
Chinese		Zai jian (Tzay Jiann)		Shi (Shyh)	Xie-Xie (Shieh-shieh)
French	Allo	Au revoir	Bon soir	Oui (Wee)	Merci
German	Hallo	Auf Wieder-sehen (owf veedersane)	Guten nacht	Ja (Ya)	Bitte
Italian	Buon giorno or Ciao	Ciao (Chow)	Buona notte	Si (See)	Grazie
Japanese		Sayonara			

Note

It is too bad that Americans are so phobic about foreign languages, since childhood is a very good time to learn languages. While teenagers and adults may learn a foreign language faster than preschool children, such children are open to acquiring language on all levels and of any sort in a way that not all older people are.

A number of parents whose native language is not English nonetheless decide to speak nothing but English to their children. They do so out of fear that their children will confuse languages. It is true that some bilingual children will mix languages at first, but as they grow older, they will sort out the languages pretty much on their own, with minimal instruction.

Furthermore, the most recent evidence on mixing languages in childhood indicates that children mix languages because they hear their parents (or other caretakers) doing so. *The most important rule to follow in rearing a child to be bilingual is to speak one language or the other one but not to engage in the kind of switching from one language to the other with children that may seem natural to do with adults.* In general, the more distinct the places, times, and people associated with different languages, the better the acquisition of those languages will be.

Bilingual parents also may hesitate to teach their children their native language because they receive outdated information, based on poorly done studies from the 1920s, that bilingual children will not perform as well as monolingual children on IQ tests or in school or that bilingual children are more prone to stuttering. More recent, more competent studies indicate that bilingual children do as well as monolingual children on IQ and achievement tests and may actually do better on tests of creativity and flexibility. Since bilingual children have two words for most concepts, they quickly learn to separate word sounds from word meaning and may show other precocious signs of a consciousness of language.

In addition to possible benefits for cognitive development, there is another very important reason why children should learn more than one language. When parents whose native language is not English do not teach a child their native language, they are laying the foundation for potential communication problems with their child. Unless they are utterly fluent in English, there may come a time when they are not able to express their feelings and thoughts adequately in English or understand their child's feelings and thoughts expressed in English.

ACTING OUT

Purpose

To teach your child the meaning of relative clauses.

Props

Your child's toys.

Game

Repeat the following sentences (and sentences like them of your own devising, appropriate for whatever toys you have available). Act out that sentence with the correct toys. Then ask your child to act out exactly what you just did. Repeat the sentence in question each time. Do as many of these sentences as seems fun, although it would be surprising if your child really enjoyed more than a half dozen at a time.

1. The frog that hops on the bunny eats the hen. (In case your child has a problem with this sentence, resort to a more straightforward version of it: The frog hops on the bunny, and the frog eats the hen. Do this for any of the following sentences that your child has a problem with.)
2. The duck that quacks at the elephant swims into the bucket.
3. The baby waves at the bear, who growls at the farmer.
4. The dog that chased the pig sits on the doll's lap.
5. The mouse that was chased by the cat jumps in your pocket.
6. Raggedy Ann jumps on the seal who was patted by Raggedy Andy.
7. The hippo that sits on the little chair squashes the rubber ducky.

8. The owl that squeaks flies into the basket.
9. Clown is bitten by the alligator, who goes after the baby chick.
10. The lamb kisses Mrs. Rabbit, who yells at Peter Rabbit.
11. The Cookie Monster steals a block from the panda bear, who stole the block from Ernie.
12. Ernie, who is singing, hugs Bert.
13. The horse that pulls the wagon knocks over the fence.
14. The cow that walks over to the feeding bin pushes the pig out of the way.
15. The little man who is riding on the train gets off and goes home.
16. The lady who is roared at by the lion runs away.
17. The big bear carries the baby bear, who was hit by the dolly.
18. The monkey who was talking on the phone pats the cat.
19. The dolly kicks the ball that was rolled by the monkey.
20. The lion who roared at the doggie sits on the elephant.
21. The dolly rides the horse that was running after the cow.
22. Ernie tickles the Cookie Monster, who was hiding under the bed.
23. Raggedy Andy, who falls off the table, covers the squirrel.
24. The car that is on top of the book chases the truck.
25. The little girl who drives the tractor runs into the barn.
26. The doll who takes off her coat puts a hat on Mr. Potato Head.

Variation

Switch roles. Encourage your child to give you complicated sentences, which you act out. If necessary, recast his simpler versions into relative clauses after you have acted out a number of the sentences in the game above.

Note

A very interesting experiment by Froma Roth showed that if you work through twenty-four sentences over three separate sessions you will significantly improve your four-year-old's ability to understand relative clauses. The experiment found that this improvement lasts for at least several weeks. If your child does make a mistake, he will tend to think that the first thing named did both actions described, a strategy that is right on many occasions but which needs correcting.

FINGERSPELL

Purpose

To give your child early practice in writing numbers and the letters of the alphabet.

Game

Make a letter or number with your fingers and have your child guess what it is. Some letters are trickier than others, but there are ways of making all of the letters and the numbers one through ten.

Variations

1. Use silverware or toothpicks or whatever is handy to form letters or numbers, and have your child guess them.
2. Your child eventually will want to take his turn forming the letters and numbers and have you guess them.

Note

Your child must be able to recognize some numbers and letters before you play this game, of course. You should form letters and

numbers that he already knows, but an occasional new one may be taught in this manner, combined with first writing the letter or number on a sheet of paper.

Your child will be able to play this game even before he is able to write letters and numbers with a pen or pencil. He will enjoy being able to do so, and you may find that you tire of the game long before he does.

ROBOT TALK

Purpose

To develop your child's ability to segment words into syllables, an ability that will make it easier for him to learn how to read.

Game

Tell your child that the two of you are going to pretend to be robots for a while, and that robots speak in a funny kind of way. Say whatever you want to your child but do it in a flat, staccato voice (robots are not emotional). For example, say something like: "We are ro bots. We will eat our break fast this morn ing. We will eat poached eggs and but ter ed toast and ba con. What do you want to drink?"

Your child then is required to give his answer in ro bot ese. Keep it up as long as your child enjoys this game.

Variation

Tap Typing: If your child is not quite capable of speaking like a robot himself, have him tap once for every syllable you speak. Say that he must "type" what you say on the pretend typewriter on the table in front of him. Have him repeat exactly what you said while he is "typing" it.

Note

One study finds that half of preschool and kindergarten children can segment words into syllables, half cannot. By first grade, ninety percent of all children are capable of doing so. Do not worry if your child does not segment words perfectly. Play the game for fun and instruction rather than testing, as always.

RITNG

Purpose

To see how much your child knows about the way words are pronounced, the relationship of pronunciation to spelling, and word boundaries.

Props

Pencil and paper.

Game

When your child has just begun to read and write the letters of the alphabet, simply ask him to write such things as notes on birthday cards to Grandma or the words of the happy birthday song or an addition to your grocery list (the latter as a great favor to you when you are busy doing something else).

Variation

Have your child write little stories of his own invention, spelling words in his own way, and make a collection of them.

Note

It may surprise you to know that many three- to six-year-old children are capable of writing, largely because they invent spellings based on the sounds of letters and the relationship between those sounds and the sounds of words. For example, "lady" may be spelled "lade." Such inventions often omit nonstressed sounds: "bent" may be spelled "bet." Words that often are used together may be written as one word, reflecting the fact that for your child they really function as one unit.

You may fear that such invented spelling will become a bad habit, interfering with the real thing. But just the opposite is likely to occur. This game gives your child practice in writing letters and a sense of the purpose of writing letters, which is likely to call his attention to the way words really are spelled.

METAPHOR GAME 1

Purpose

To encourage creativity with language.

Props

A clown puppet named Gonzo and a collection of odds and ends such as you would find in a "junk" drawer in your kitchen. Objects with only loosely defined functions, such as blocks or sponges, prompt more metaphors than ones with familiar, well-defined functions, such as can openers.

Game

Ask your child to have Gonzo the puppet give a pretend name for each object. If your child comes up with a real name, acknowledge that that is the right name for the object, but ask him for a pretend name. If, for example, your child calls a seashell a "hat" or a "bowl," say "That's a good pretend name for this shell. Then make an appropriate motion with the object (put the "hat" on his head or pretend to eat out of the "bowl").

If he still draws a blank, move the object around to give him a hint. For example, sniff a glass-cleaning sponge to elicit the name "flower." Or put a paper clip on your finger to elicit the name "ring," or make a green block hop around to elicit the name "frog."

Variations

1. Encourage a whole set of objects to be involved in the same game of pretend naming. For example, say "Let's make an elf house out of these things. We'll pretend this (eraser) is a sink. What do you think these (nails) are?"

2. Have your child complete sentences such as the following:

a. Things don't have to be huge in size to look that way. Look at that boy standing over there. He looks as gigantic as _____.

b. Sometimes things seem loud even if they are making no noise. Look at that dress. It looks as loud as _____.

c. Some things seem cold even if they don't feel cold. What about the man in his picture? He looks as cold as _____.

3. Borrow or buy a copy of *Quick as a Cricket* by Audrey Wood (Child's Play Ltd.), one of the few books I have found that recognizes a child's ability to enjoy figurative language. It depicts a series of similes such as "I'm as mean as a shark," and "I'm as hot as a fox." Take off from the book, saying, "I think you're funny, as funny as a _____ (ask him to complete the sentence). Or "I think your skin is soft, as soft as _____." Or, "I think your muscles are hard, as hard as _____."

METAPHOR GAME 2

Purpose

To encourage creativity with language and expression of feelings.

Game

Ask your child the following set of questions from time to time, as well as others like these:

> Could the sun smile? When?
> Could the sun sing? How?
> Could the sky shout? How?
> Could the sky cry? When?
> Could the moon yawn? When?
> Could a person be warm? How?
> Could a person be hard? How?
> Could a color be loud? Which color?

Variations

1. Instead of giving your child a comparison and asking him to come up with the way two different things could be related, give him the way two things could be related along with one of the things and ask him to name another. Here you are looking for less literal comparisons than in Variation 1 of Metaphor Game 1. For example, ask the following questions:

a. If I were in a bad mood, I might say that I am as sour as a _____.

b. If I were feeling really smart one day, I might say that I am as bright as a _____.

c. If the mailman were very nice to me, smiling and bringing my mail all the way to our door, I might say that he was as warm as a _____.

d. When it is Christmas Eve and you get all excited about Santa Claus coming, you could say that you are as high as a _____.

e. If my best friend cheated in a card game with me, I would be as bitter as a _____.

f. If you felt very proud about being brave in a doctor's office, you could say that you felt as big as a _____.

g. If you helped me set the table when I was in a big hurry and you did a good job, I would say you were as sweet as a _____.

h. If your teacher were very strict and wouldn't let you talk to your friends at all, you would say he was as hard as a _____.

i. But if your teacher let you play outside as much as you wanted to and let you talk to your friends as much as you wanted to, you would say she was as soft as a _____.

j. If you felt sad because your best friend moved away, you might say that you were as low as a _____.

CLOUD GAME

Purpose

To encourage creative naming.

Game

Take any set of things that vary in shape and take turns naming them. Say, "That cloud looks like a fish to me, what does it look like to you?" You can play this game with imprints in the sand or splotches of paint on clothing or orange peels or scraps of torn wrapping paper. The first person who cannot think of a good name gets a monster kiss (blowing out on their forehead).

Variations

1. Each person has to explain *how* the object in question looks like a fireplug or a kite or what have you. Whoever cannot explain one of their names gets a monster kiss.

2. In an art museum, ask your child to name an abstract painting and to explain why he has named it as such. Praise him

for his efforts, especially if he came up with a good name and explained it well. After that, explain what the artist named the painting and why you think she or he did so. Remember that the process is more important than the results at this age, so do not be too concerned about your abilities as an art critic. Just enjoy yourselves.

Note

A necklace makes a good object with which to play this game. Take turns with your child changing the shape of the necklace and naming it.

IT LOOKS LIKE A COW, BUT IT'S REALLY A LOG

Purpose

Although at first this may seem like Cloud Game, the purpose of this language game is just the opposite of that one. Whereas the purpose of Cloud Game was to encourage creative naming by pointing out the similarities between things, the purpose of this game is just the opposite: to train a child to notice the *differences* between appearances and reality.

Game

This is a good car game. As you are driving along, point out things in the distance, saying what they look like from afar, and then, of course, name what they look like up close. The more you play this game, the better you will get at coming up with guesses about things you truly do not recognize from a distance. Kites may turn out to be parachutes, stars turn out to be plane lights, puddles on hot roads turn out to be mirages, etc. You can call these events "tricks."

Variation

Encourage your child to come up with "tricks." Give each person playing a point for coming up with a good "trick." See who has the most "tricks" at the end of the car ride.

Note

Many people are familiar with Piaget's notion that children are unable to conserve. That is, Piaget demonstrated that before the age of seven, children think that an amount of liquid changes if it is poured into a different shape of glass. He felt that children just would grow naturally out of this way of thinking in the course of their normal interaction with the world around them. However, some research indicates that this sort of game can speed up your child's ability to conserve by showing how frequently perceptual appearances are deceiving. Most three-year-olds will have a tough time with this game, but they will improve as they approach five.

OPPOSITES

Purpose

To play up the relationship between words and their opposites.

Props

A dictionary may be needed.

Game

This game requires at least three people, including one moderator who gives the words, and two players. More players are welcome and will add excitement. The game consists of the moderator giving words for which an antonym is needed. Whoever shouts out the best antonym first gets a point. Play until someone reaches fifty points. There will be ties. There also will be debates about which word is the best opposite for a particular word. Debates should be resolved by consulting a dictionary of synonyms and antonyms or a regular dictionary. Antonyms that consist of "not" plus the word should not count unless no one can think of any other antonym. For example, "nasty" is a better antonym of "nice" than "not nice" for this game.

Variations

1. For older, school-aged children: If the game gets too wild or there are too many ties for first or someone is too shy to shout out answers, you may want to have each person write down an antonym and see who has the best word. Consult a dictionary to determine this, because you may be surprised at the exact meanings of even the most common words (see "nice" for example).

2. A simpler version of this game can be played with only two players—you and your child. Think up a word and its opposite and have your child guess the opposite. If he cannot think of the word, you win that round. If he comes up with the antonym, he wins.

3. Once children have a good understanding of opposites, you might suggest that you all play "Opposite Day." On Opposite Day, you say things like, "Isn't it hot outside?" when snow is falling. Your child calls his mother "Daddy" and his father "Mommy." You say that you hate chicken soup, which he knows to be your favorite and so on. I have observed children about five or six years to start such games themselves.

TURN ABOUT

Purpose

To see how you communicate with your child and to show her how she communicates with you.

Game

Switch roles with your child while going to bed or eating dinner. Pretend to be your child and have your child pretend to be you. Notice what your child does. Does she nag you? Does she scold you a lot? Does she compliment you? Does she hug you? Whatever you do, *do not criticize or even comment on how she portrays you*. Just file her portrait away for your own information. If she scolds you a lot, perhaps you *are* scolding her more than you intend to. If so, see Big Girls Don't Cry and other language games to use as a substitute for scolding. A number of games are designed to distract a child from mischief (including What If?, Pat Your Head, etc.), and all language games are designed to encourage communication.

Variations

1. Instead of playing this game in real settings, play it about pretend settings. Good ones to try are riding in the car, going to the doctor's office, teaching something (e.g., how to tie a shoelace).
2. Play this game with puppets. You manipulate the child puppet, while your child uses the parent puppet.

Note

This game is inspired by exercises some clinical psychologists use to treat patients. They play the game to hold up a psychological mirror to each person involved, a mirror comprised of other players' portrayals, but they also play it for other reasons. My point in mentioning this is to say that you can find out useful information from playing this game. However, if you feel anxious or notice that your child feels anxious during the game, or if you feel tempted to scold your child for playing "parent" in some way, STOP THE GAME. If you truly feel that you and your child have problems communicating, consider consulting a psychologist. Many parents compulsively take their child to medical doctors every time they have a virus even though they know very well that the doctor will tell them there is nothing to be done about a virus except bed rest, chicken soup, and cough medicine. But the same parents agonize about or refuse outright to consult with a psychologist. Many huge problems between parents and children *can* be solved at low cost and with relative ease if they are caught early enough.

For most parents and children, however, this game simply will be fun. Children will enjoy the chance to boss their parents around for a little while. Parents will enjoy being tucked into bed or otherwise taken care of by their children for a change. As always, play this game for fun, not for instruction or self-therapy.

✳ 7 ✳

Transition to School:
Five to Seven Years

Development continues on all levels during this age range. As far as vocabulary goes, some researchers estimate that the average six-year-old knows perhaps several thousand words. Do not be afraid to use advanced vocabulary with your kindergartner, provided you explain the words you use in terms she can understand.

Development also occurs in sentence construction. There has been much research on the issue of when young children understand passive sentences, and the upshot of all that research is very complicated. Three- and four-year-old children typically rely on the order of words to understand sentences: "The truck was pushed by the car" is usually—(but not always)—interpreted to mean that the truck pushes the car. Children may understand passive sentences depending on a host of factors, including whether or not the subject of a passive sentence is the focus of their attention, whether the sentence is equally plausible as an active and passive sentence, or whether or not they are holding whatever serves as the subject of the sentence. The process of understanding passive sentences seems to begin at about four years but may not be complete until almost thirteen years of age. The Cookies Were

Eaten by Greg deals with continuing improvement in understanding complex sentences.

Perhaps the most dramatic language development at this time will be your child's ability at the age of six or so to tell a good narrative about what has happened to her. Cartoon Sort works with improving the ability to sequence events in a story, one of the prerequisites for telling narratives at school. Carole Peterson and I have found that children go through several stages in telling their narratives. They begin narrating personal events at about age two and a half, when they are regularly producing sentences that consist of more than one word. At first, their narratives will be only a few words long, such as "Beth . . . crayons," a narrative a two-year-old came up with in response to a school picture of Beth. (She was referring to the time she had colored with Beth several months previously.) But by three and a half years, children are putting more than one sentence together to talk about experiences they have had. Three- and four-year-olds typically will tend to leap around through a series of more-or-less related actions, as in the following narrative:

> ADULT: I used to go on trips to Cleveland to see the zoo. Have you ever been to Oberlin or Cleveland or any place like that?
> CHILD: I been, been to, to Cooper's right there.
> ADULT: You've been where?
> CHILD: Cooper's house. Sometimes.
> ADULT: And?
> CHILD: I just said, I, I said, "Hi, hello, and how are you?" And then, and then, they go to someplace else and then, and then I had a party, with, with, with candy and . . . hmm . . . my, and my, um I don't know.
> ADULT: And you what?
> CHILD: I don't know what I did. I *sure* had a party.
>   (Told by a four-year-old girl.)

After enough parental questions about the confusion that

abounds in narratives like the previous one, five-year-olds are somewhat more organized:

> ADULT: I had a cold and I had to go to the doctor's. She gave me some big pink pills that I had to take. Did you ever go to the doctor's office?
>
> CHILD: Uh-uh. No, yes, over Dr. Garth's house, night.
>
> ADULT: You went there? What happened?
>
> CHILD: Nothing. Just I sticked around and he told me to come in first, and then he, and, that's all I had to do. And taked me out, out, and had he put me in the doctor office. And I had a cold.
>
> ADULT: You did?
>
> CHILD: Last night.
>
> ADULT: Right.
>
> CHILD: And I, I was scared to come in. And he didn't shot me or nothing.
>
> ADULT: He didn't shot you or anything?
>
> CHILD: Uh-uh. He didn't even shot me.
>
> ADULT: He didn't shoot you?
>
> CHILD: He gave me them, them tiny pills too, just like you. That's only reason I had.
>
> (Told by a five-year-old boy.)

This narrative follows an orderly progression of events, leading up to and ending at the most important event: the doctor did not give the child a shot.

After another year of questioning, six-year-olds typically tell a narrative in complete adult form. They give a series of events that lead up to the most important event, dwell on that event for a while, and then go on to tell how things were resolved, as in the following narrative:

> CHILD: I'm, we're lucky we have a big closet.
>
> ADULT: Uh huh.
>
> CHILD: We're lucky we have a shelf way up high. Once Mom-

my said, "Why'nt you just dust." And so I got up on that, this doll pan, to get polish and a rag. We were polishing and Mommy forgot there was a mouse trap up there. There wasn't a mouse in it, and guess what? I reached up there and my thumb got caught in it.

ADULT: Your thumb got caught in it?

CHILD: (Giggles) It really scared me. I jumped off the stool. (Laughs) Then I went over. Mommy said, "Oh, I'm sorry, I forgot there was one there." (Giggles) That did hurt, too.

(Told by a six-year-old girl.)

This girl tells you the events leading up to the most important event—getting her finger caught in the mousetrap—but she also tells you events that came after that central event, such as her frightened reaction and her mother's apology.

Children talk increasingly about the goals that people set for themselves and their attempts to reach those goals. In the four-year-old's narrative about the party, all we get is a list of more-or-less related actions, with no inkling of why people were doing what they were doing. In the five-year-old's narrative about going to the doctor's office, we also have a series of actions more clearly related to each other, along with the narrator's reactions to what happened. But it is only in the third narrative—the six-year-old's narrative about dusting—that the child clearly articulates her goal (and her mother's) of getting polish and a rag in order to dust.

This is also a special time in your child's language development because she is just about ready to learn to read and is working on many skills that will be used in reading, skills such as classifying objects and hooking up speech sounds to print that can be exercised in the following language games. Words That Begin with B and For the Record develop skills that are necessary for reading. Be sure to continue playing previous reading-readiness games such as Rhymes, Robot Talk, and RITNG. By the end of this period, your child will be able to read some words and simple stories.

You can observe the development of reading readiness in

your child when you play For the Record, a game in which your child dictates stories to you. (I am indebted to Elizabeth Sulzby for the following descriptions.) In this game, your child at first will not understand that you need time to write, and she probably will tell the story to you just as fast as if you were not writing. You will need to interrupt her to slow her down. Point to what you have written to draw her attention to the reason for the interruptions.

You probably will find that after such interruptions your child will simply take up where she left off, not giving you the information you missed. Or she will give you a different version of the missed information or even an entirely new set of ideas altogether. Very young children who have no clear idea of written language do all these things.

If you play the game again months later, however, you may find that your child has developed a clearer sense of written language and that she marks this by telling you the story word by word, pausing for several seconds between each word—almost annoyingly slowly. The following is an example of what this stage sounds like:

There (4 second pause)
was (3 second pause)
a little boy (5 second pause)
and (3 second pause)
his (3 second pause)
friend (5 second pause)
and (4 second pause)
they were (5 second pause)
planning (5 second pause)
a race. (4 second pause)
So (3 second pause)
he (4 second pause)
put (3 second pause)
down (3 second pause)
some (4 second pause)
tape (4 second pause)

and he (3 second pause)
had (3 second pause)
a (2 second pause)
race. (6 second pause)
      (Told by a girl toward the end of her kindergarten year.)

You hope that your child does not have a very long story in mind at this stage, given how slowly she is telling it. Be patient, though. Recognize this as progress in understanding that written language is a way of communicating and has rules that are different from speaking. It is a stage that typically does not last too long.

Eventually your child will have a much better idea of how much time you need to write things down, and she will pause between ideas rather than at the end of virtually every word. At this point, your child is probably very ready to read. Children who are ready to read adapt their dictation to suit the needs of the person who is writing.

Individual differences at this age are readily apparent in the types of narratives children produce. I believe that one of the most important ways we get to know other people is through their personal narratives. Unfortunately, many people never develop much skill in narrating, possibly because they were never encouraged to do so. Compare the following two narratives (this discussion of narratives is taken from a book I wrote with Carole Peterson, titled *Developmental Psycholinguistics*):

ADULT: Once I went swimming in the ocean and got jabbed by a spiny urchin needle in my hand. Have you ever gotten jabbed with anything?
CHILD: By a bee.
ADULT: By a bee? Oh, tell me about it.
CHILD: It got kind of cool one day and my grandma came. She called me and she wanted to know where Dennis was.
ADULT: Where Dennis was?

CHILD: Yeah, and I ran outside to tell her and I was running and I stepped on a bee.

ADULT: You went outside to tell her and you were running and you stepped on a bee. Then what?

CHILD: Nothing. I just went in the house and had to have something on it.

(Told by an eight-year-old girl.)

ADULT: (Same narrative) Have you ever gotten jabbed with anything?

CHILD: Uh huh. I got jabbed with a bee.

ADULT: By a bee? Oh, tell me about it.

CHILD: See, I got jabbed on my foot. I was barefooted. I screamed and I screamed and I cried and I cried. I screamed and I *screamed*. Until my next door neighbor came out and my dad came out and my brother came out. And they *all* carried me into the house, but after that happened I got to sleep overnight with my neighbor.

(Told by a five-year-old girl.)

The second child clearly tells her listener about how much she had suffered during the experience, and she is typical. The first child was the only one we ever came across who did not evaluate her experience in any way. That is the difference between the two narratives: the second one tells you what the narrator's feelings were, whereas the first does not. The expression of feelings is a common part of most narratives and provides invaluable information for parents who really want to know their child.

I have collected some favorite narratives over the years, like the one from a little boy who tried to convince me that he held up a tree that had fallen on his house "with my pinky." Or the one from another youngster who told us about how his sister had hit him with "a hard, hard, sharp, sharp broom" before he retaliated and hit her back with a rake so hard that he sent her to the hospital for stitches. You may enjoy some of your children's narratives so much that you write them down, word for word (see For the Record), or record them on a tape recorder. I think of narratives as treasure chests filled with gems like the exaggerations I just mentioned, along with a child's view of various characters, and sometimes such cute comments like, "Don't ever take a little annarule (animal) by my dog or he will eat it up," or "And this is where my brother was appetized."

In addition to individual differences in narrative style, there also seem to be cultural differences. For example, Courtney Cazden and Sarah Miles have found that some black children tell narratives that are more like a series of thematically related events than stories with a clear beginning, middle, and end. It is important to develop an appreciation for cultural and individual differences in storytelling.

Relating events that happened in the past requires that a child remember them, and, in a variety of ways, your child's memory will be improving during this period. For one thing, her working memory will expand. By working memory, I mean the type of memory you use when you look up a phone number and repeat it over and over to yourself until you dial the number, after which you usually forget it as your attention turns to your discussion with the person you have called. Much research has shown that adults can keep approximately seven things in working memory. You can remember seven numbers or letters or words at a time, usually by repeating these things over and over and over. Children cannot keep as many things in mind. A three-year-old usually can keep only one to three things in working memory. A four- or five-year-old child can usually keep three or four things in mind at one time. A seven- or eight-year-old can manage four or five things. There are individual differences in the span of working memory.

Memory is not a machine. That is, children do not come with good or bad memories the way that we buy good or bad flashlights, tape recorders, and the like. Remembering things takes work and technique. You can improve your child's memory by understanding this and by working with her to improve it.

I have included a couple of games designed to improve your child's memory, something that is as important as reading for success in school. Grocery Store and Pat Your Head, Stick Out Your Tongue, Scratch Your Back, and Untie Your Shoe are games that require remembering. Demanding that your child remember things is the best way to improve her memory. Grocery Store has one very important rule, which requires your child to repeat what is said to her at last three times. Repeating items that are to be remembered is a basic technique for improving memory, and it is important to get your child used to using it.

In other areas of cognitive development, your child will also change dramatically during this age range. At seven, she will be capable of much more planning than she was at five. At seven or shortly thereafter, she will understand fully how to arrange things in serial order. At this age, seven, she will be much more likely to do things out of a sense of pride rather than for some external reward.

These cognitive changes have a dramatic impact on perhaps the major emotional accomplishment during this time, namely, the development of the ability to understand death. Recall that at three, your child developed the ability to understand and cope with separations from you, largely because she could understand that you were going some specific place from which you would return at some specific time. In other words, she learned that temporary separations from her loved ones were reversible. However, for a while, what enabled her to deal with temporary separation got in the way of her ability to understand final separation in the form of death. After the death of her great-grandmother, one three-year-old said, "When is she going to come back and be a grandmother again?" She did not yet understand that death is irreversible. Her great-grandmother had been ill for a long time prior to dying and had been hospitalized. This three-year-old girl tended to associate death with scary but curable illness and would speak of her great-grandmother when she herself was coming down with a sore throat, for example. By seven, most children will have corrected these misconceptions about death. They will understand that dead people cannot become alive again.

Carole Peterson and I found that children rarely talk about deaths of pets or people before the age of five, but readily do so thereafter. However, even though most seven-year-olds understand the concept of death, there are limits to the maturity of their talk about it. Between the ages of five and nine, children tend to recount only the facts about some death that has involved them. They rarely mention any feelings for the dead pet or person, even if that person was a parent. In fact, their narratives sound like recapitulations of television plots, simple laundry lists of events. At nine, children mention feelings for dead pets, but not for relatives who have died. The closer the person who has died, the less likely they are to express feelings about them. These children seem to be distancing themselves from their feelings for their lost loved ones. They are talking in a detached way about these lost people, just as two-year-olds act detached when confronted with attachment figures who in their view have abandoned them for too long. Of course, in contrast to children, the closer the person who has died, the more feelings adults express for them in the normal course of grieving.

A full account of how children grieve and how you should handle their grief is beyond the scope of this book. Suffice it to say that should the occasion arise, and our research indicates that for most children it will, you should talk to your child openly and freely as much as she wants to talk about the death, and she will want to talk about it. The Tell a Story to Get a Story game that you began to play when your child was three should prove useful in this respect.

Many games in this section are just for fun. Although you will find yourself no longer talking Toddler Talk to your child, most language games you have learned in previous sections will still be fun. The games in this section that I consider the most important for general cognitive development are What Do You Hear?, Grocery Store, Pat Your Head, etc., Cartoon Sort, Words That Begin with *B*, For the Record, and Points of View.

WHAT DO YOU HEAR?

Purpose

To encourage your child to observe with her ears, nose, tongue, and sense of touch as well as with her eyes.

Props

Anything handy.

Game

This is a good game to play while waiting in airports, bus stations, or the doctor's office. Have your child shut her eyes and tell you everything she hears. Have her open her eyes and see how right she was.

Variations

1. Try having your child shut her eyes and describe everything she smells. You could put such things as perfume, food, spices, and toys in front of her and have her guess what they are. This version is best played at home.

2. Try the same game with tasting. Have your child close her eyes and guess what food she is tasting. This version is best played at dinner time, but it may be hard to get started if your child is a picky eater, unwilling to be adventuresome while eating.

3. Try the game with the sense of touch. Have your child close her eyes. Put something in her hands and have her guess what it is. This is a good version for waiting rooms, and your purse or pocket provides a good collection of things to guess by touching.

4. Try the guess-what-you-hear game, but this time both of you play. Take turns naming something you hear. The first person who cannot hear something new gets tickled. (You will amaze

yourself at how much there is to hear in any situation, even one in which people are supposed to be quiet, such as in a waiting room.)

Note

This game can help shift your child's attention away from misbehaving by calling attention to all the interesting things around her at any particular time. If played often enough, it will help your child to become much more observant of the world around her, a skill that is useful no matter what she goes on to do with her life (see Describe It, pp. 212–213).

WHAT'S THE FIRST THING YOU THINK OF?

Purpose

To discover your child's thoughts about different things.

Game

Simply name something and ask your child what pops into her mind. Make sure she responds with a single word. Ask her to explain why she thought of what she did. Examples: water, bedtime, night, father, mother, grandma, car, goodbye, ice cream, baby. Never criticize or correct your child for thinking what she does about things. If you do criticize her, you can expect that she will never play the game freely with you again. Everyone has a right to think what they do. You are trying just to discover what your child thinks, not change it. Or at least, do not try to change what she thinks while you are playing this game.

Variations

1. Ask your child to name the first and then the second thing she thinks of when you say the word in question. Then the third,

the fourth, and so on. After she stops thinking of things, talk about why she thought of what she did. Do not talk about any of the things she says until she finishes naming things. Repeat the word you are focusing on each time, otherwise your child is likely to go off on a tangent.

2. When your child can write, ask her to write down the things of which she thinks, while you do the same. Compare your lists and discuss them.

Notes

This game is based on the technique known as free association, popularized by Sigmund Freud. Freud had his patients free associate to things they dreamed about so that he could discover what those things meant to them.

This is a game that can be played throughout life, but note that children change the sort of associations they will have. At first, children are likely to form phrases, such as responding to "dog" with "barking." Later, they are increasingly likely to respond with words similar in kind to the focus word, such as responding to "dog" with "cat" or "log."

In elementary school, you can begin to teach your child something about the way to understand good poetry and fiction by asking her to free associate to key words. Why did Beatrix Potter compare Peter Rabbit's eyes to lollipops in *Benjamin Bunny?* Because candy makes children (and grown-ups, for that matter) think of sweetness and good things, taking the edge off the scary situation Peter finds himself in at the time in Mr. McGregor's garden.

GROCERY STORE

Purpose

To develop your child's memory.

Props

Toy cash register and grocery cart, play money, pretend or real food. There are bags of pretend groceries available in most dime stores. If you don't have groceries, substitute toys and play Toy Store instead.

Game

Set up "groceries." Across the room from them, read a list of things your child must buy at the store. Give her a cart or basket to put the purchases in and "money" with which to pay for them. The child has to go to the groceries, select them, and bring them back to the cash register, where you play salesclerk. Afterward, check your list with what she "bought" and let her know how proud you are that she remembered. Require your child to repeat over and over the items she is supposed to "buy." This repetition rule is the most important rule of the game because it is teaching the child a basic strategy for remembering things. By the way, if she forgets, give her a hint such as "It started with the letter *A*."

Variation

Play the game with a group of children. Have one child play salesclerk and the rest play shoppers. Give individual lists. The one who remembers the most items wins.

PAT YOUR HEAD, STICK OUT YOUR TONGUE, SCRATCH YOUR BACK, AND UNTIE YOUR SHOE

Purpose

To develop your child's memory.

Game

This is a good game to play in the car or on a plane. Give your child a series of actions to do. She must do exactly what you say in the exact order that you say it. For example, ask her to "roll your eyes, snap your fingers three times, shuffle your feet, make a fist, and cross your legs." This game differs from Do What I Say (see pp. 69–70) in that your child cannot begin to carry out the actions until you have finished talking. In other words, the earlier game involves learning and playing with action words, while this game involves memory.

Variations

1. Play the game with more than one child, ages three on up. Adapt your series of instructions for each child's age (see Note). Take turns giving each child a series of instructions that are different each time. Every time a child completes one series successfully, give him or her one point. The child with the most points wins a prize. For example, tell your four-year-old to rub her belly, clap her hands, and blow a kiss. If she does it correctly, give her a point. Then tell your six-year-old to stamp his foot, cluck four times, nod his head once, and wink. If he does it correctly, give him a point. Give your nine-year-old five or six things to do in order to earn one point, and so forth.

2. Have each child request a number of actions. Give children points for every action they request and do correctly, but take points away for every action they request that they do not do correctly. For example, if a child asks for nine actions, of which she remembers only five, she gets five points minus four points (for the four requested but forgotten actions). So she only ends up with one point, whereas a child who only asked for two actions but did them both correctly would end up with two. Again, the child with the most points wins. This variation encourages a child to recognize her own limitations.

Note

This exercise shifts giving orders from nagging to playing a fun game that actually may benefit your child if it is played often enough. It is a good way to control your child who occasionally has a lot of energy and no place to vent it.

Researchers also have found a developmental shift related to Variation 2. If you ask children ages three to five how many items on a list they think they will be able to recall, they are likely to say "everything." Older children are much more realistic in their expectations. However, there is some evidence that five-year-olds can become more realistic about how well they will do provided that they are given a series of tests, such as Variation 2 involves. This greater realism about their abilities in turn may prompt them to work harder at remembering things. And working hard to remember things is what makes for a good memory at any age.

DRRRACULAAAA

Purpose

To enjoy using theatrical language with your child.

Props

None are necessary, but you may want to use two towels as capes.

Game

Pretend to be Dracula, talking more or less as he would: "I am zee Count Drrrraculaaa and I vill get you velly soooooon. I only come out in zee night time and I like to kiss you on your neck velllly much. Cooooome here my dahlink. . . ." Your child should pretend to be another vampire, speaking as vampires might.

Variation

Try talking like an alien from another planet, with no emotion at all in your voice. "We come from Mars. We want to look at magazine. We want to see pictures. See that thing right there. . . ." Again, encourage your child to talk the same way.

Note

I find this game fun to play anytime, but it is also especially useful when you have reached a stalemate with your child and want to get her to do something. She might not want to pick up her room if you, her obnoxious parent, ask her, but she might have a good time doing it at Dracula's suggestion.

YOU ARE AN UMBRELLA

Purpose

To encourage your child, while teasing her, to see the similarities and differences between things.

Game

Playfully call your child something, for example, an umbrella. She says, "No, I am not an umbrella." You say, "Oh, yes, you are an umbrella because you open up when it rains the way an umbrella does." She says, "I am not." You say, "Oh yes, you are an umbrella because sometimes you stand in the corner the way an umbrella does." She says, "But I'm people and an umbrella isn't." You say, "Okay, you win."

Or you say, "You're a bird, you know." She says, "No, I'm not." You say, "Oh yes, you are because you have two legs the way a bird does." She says, "I am not a bird." You say, "Oh yes, you are a bird because you have two eyes the way a bird does." She says, "I am not a bird because birds have beaks." You say, "Okay, you win. You aren't a bird after all because you don't have a beak and a bird does."

Variation

Instead of having your child come up with the differences, have your child come up with the similarities. Ask your child how she could be like a steamroller ("I smash things that get in my way") or a dog ("I bark") or a petunia ("I am purple" or "I like the sun"), and so on.

WHAT GALLOPS?

Purpose

To focus your child's attention on verbs and to determine if she knows which nouns typically go with certain verbs.

Game

Ask your child what typically does a series of actions. For example, ask her if she knows what gallops, what runs, what bites, what sews, what flies, what swims, what eats, what brays, what snorts, and so forth. Some verbs, such as "runs," can go with a lot of nouns, while others, such as "brays," typically go with only a few. If your child says something that seems strange, such as "machines bite," ask her what she means. If she says, for example, "Well, the sewing machine bit you," meaning that your finger got caught in the sewing machine the other day, tell her that people usually do not think of machines as biting, that usually we think of only animals as biting, but that that was a good pretend way of saying something.

Variations

1. Think of something specific that bites, for example. Have your child go through a number of things that typically bite until she guesses the one that you are thinking of.
2. Play Variation 1 but switch roles. Have your child think of something that bites while you try to guess it.

WUGS

Purpose

To show your child (and you) how much she already knows about grammar.

Props

Pencil and paper.

Game

Draw silly pictures depicting the following things or act them out yourself. Say the sentences, but let your child fill in the italicized word. You may be surprised to learn how well your child can derive the correct forms of words when she has never heard the exact forms.

1. Present progressive: When I move my finger this way, I say that I mook. If I keep it up, I say that I am *mooking*.
2. Plural: If this is one wug, then these are two *wugs*.
3. Possessive: If this is a gorpok and this ball belongs to the gorpok, we would say that this ball is the *gorpok's*. This budgie bird belongs to me. This budgie bird is *mine*.
4. Articles: This is *a* nubbock. If I lost him, I would ask you where is *which* nubbock? Right, *the* nubbock.
5. Regular past tense: This is a woman who knows how to

melish. She is melishing right now. What did she do yesterday? Yesterday, she *melished*.

6. Third person present tense, regular: Yesterday, Kim smooshed and today she will do the same thing. What does Kim do? She *smooshes*.
7. Auxiliary: This man knows how to blick. In this picture, what is he doing? He *is blicking* or *He's blicking*.
8. Verb to noun transformation: If this man blicks, he must be a *blicker*.

Variation

Use Lewis Carroll's poem "Jabberwocky," asking your child such questions as: What would more than one Jabberwock (or bandersnatch) be called? If the vorpol blade went snicker-snack yesterday, tomorrow the vorpol blade *will go snicker-snack*.

Notes

Jean Berko Gleason invented this game to show that children were acquiring rules when they learned language rather than simply parroting their parents. Preschool and first-grade children are capable of coming up with the correct forms of words even before they hear those exact forms because they extend grammatical rules to new words. In fact, this is the very positive ability that causes them to make such "mistakes" as "He runned away" or "I hi-ed the man." The items in this game are arranged from least to most difficult. Make up new nonsense words each time you play the game.

THE COOKIES WERE EATEN BY GREG

Purpose

To teach your child the meaning of passive sentences.

Props

Toys to act out the following scenes: Scene 1 calls for a crumb of cheese, an aunt doll, a mouse, a cat, a dog, and some cookies (in a plastic cup "cookie jar"). Scene 2 calls for a Raggedy Andy doll (or some other doll), mother and father dolls, a shopping cart, and some things (real or pretend) to put in the cart. Scene 3 is to be played before bathtime and requires a plastic or stuffed bee, a plastic car, a cow, a rabbit, a lamb, a fish, a boat, and a figure of a woman such as you find in the Fisher-Price farm family; you also need a ruler and a block to set up as a seesaw. Place a rubber band around the lamb and put it on one end of the "seesaw."

Game

Using toys, act out the events in the following scenes:

Scene 1: Who ate the cookies?
     Well, it all started when a crumb of cheese was dropped on the floor by Aunt Sarah.
     Later that night, the crumb of cheese was eaten by a little gray mouse.
     And the cat was awakened by the little gray mouse.
     The little gray mouse was chased by the cat.
     The dog was tripped over and awakened by the cat.
     The cat was chased by the dog.
     The cookie jar was knocked over by the cat.
     Greg (child's name) was awakened by the noise.
     The mess had to be cleaned up by someone.
     Soooo . . . .
     The cookies were eaten by . . . Greg, who was just trying to help. (If you are using real cookies as props here, you might let your child eat them.)

Scene 2: Who broke the pickle jar?
     Once upon a time, Raggedy Andy was taken grocery shopping by his parents.

He was put into a shopping cart and pushed around the store by his father.

He was given a loaf of bread to hold by his mother.

Some jelly was put in the shopping cart.

An apple was put in the shopping cart.

A box of cereal was put in the shopping cart.

A mouse, sleeping behind the cereal, was pushed into the cart by the little boy's mother.

The mouse was discovered in his shirt by Raggedy Andy.

The bread was thrown by Raggedy Andy.

Sooo . . . .

The pickle jar was hit and broken by the loaf of bread.

Scene 3: Who knocked over the woman? (To be played just before bath time.)

One afternoon, Queen Buzzy Bee was run into by a car.

A cow was chased by Queen Buzzy Bee.

A rabbit was pushed by the frightened cow.

A seesaw was jumped on by the rabbit.

A lamb was tossed into the air by the seesaw.

The water was jumped into by the lamb. (This move may require some practice.)

A fish was frightened by the splash.

A boat was jumped into by the fish.

And. . . .

The woman on the boat was knocked over by the fish. . . .

And the splash and the lamb and the seesaw and the rabbit and the cow and Queen Buzzy Bee and a car.

Variation

After you have acted out the scenes, let your child act them out. Repeat each passive construction a number of times, showing your child the right way to act it out if she makes a mistake.

Note

This game is designed to give your child concentrated experience in hearing the passive construction. The scenes suggested also play up a reason for using that awkward, difficult construction: it makes whoever does the action described seem less powerful and, consequently, less to blame for something.

CARTOON SORT

Purpose

To encourage your child to tell the events of a story in chronological order.

Props

Newspaper cartoons.

Game

Take a cartoon your child enjoys, cut it into individual frames, and jumble it up. Hand the jumbled stack of frames to your child and ask her to arrange it in the right order and tell you the story of what is going on. The first few times you play this game, you should read your child the story before you cut up the cartoon and ask her to rearrange it. Also, begin with a cartoon that consists of only three or four frames.

Variations

1. After your child becomes adept at arranging cartoons you have read to her first, cut up a cartoon before she reads it to see if she can figure out what is going on. Have her arrange the pictures and then tell the story.

2. When sorting three or four frames presents no difficulty for

your child, use cartoons consisting of more frames. Increase the task just a few frames at a time.

Note

This game is derived from a task that often is found on intelligence tests for children, so by playing it you will be giving your child practice with an important skill in a relaxed setting. Do not expect your child to become proficient at this task until the end of this age range.

WORDS THAT BEGIN WITH *B*

Purpose

To focus your child's attention on the letters that make up a word in order to promote spelling skills.

Game

Take turns naming words that begin with some letter of the alphabet. The first one who cannot think of a new word or who names a word that does not begin with the correct letter gets tickled. Proper names and repeats (such as "button" and "buttons" or "run" and "running") do not count.

Variation

Have your child name all the words that begin with a certain letter in one minute's time. Count how many she names correctly. Keep track to see if she can beat her old record.

FOR THE RECORD

Purpose

To teach your child about written language and to find out how much she already knows. Variation 1 may develop reading skills.

Game

Even before children learn to read, they form an idea of written language. How much they understand will become clear in the following game, which is a simple one. Have your child draw a picture and then tell you a story about that picture while you record the story. The story could be about something that really happened or about a make-believe event. Interrupt your child to slow her down if necessary, drawing attention to words you have written. Read her story back to her when you are finished, pointing to each word as you read it.

Variations

1. Let kindergarten children "read" back their own stories after they are written down.

2. If you have a group of children, have them take turns making up a joint story (real or make-believe). Each child adds one sentence at a time. Stop them if they continue past one sentence. They may not understand what "one sentence" means.

Note

This game is adapted from research done by Elizabeth Sulzby.

In Variation 1, you are asked to have your child "read" what she has "written" to see if it is recorded exactly as she wants it. Some teachers argue. that children will learn to read more easily from their own language about familiar topics than they will from books written by others.

At the end of this game, you have a picture and a story in your child's own words—a wonderful souvenir of your child's growing up. What better present for a doting grandmother than a book about a visit to her house?

Note that, in general, this language game will not produce stories as good as the ones produced in Tell a Story to Get a Story because the child is slowing down, attending to "writing" rather than telling. But it will both reflect your child's knowledge of written language and instruct her further about it.

POINTS OF VIEW

Purpose

To encourage your child to think about events from different perspectives.

Props

Your child's books.

Game

After you finish reading a book, ask your child to describe how each character felt. For example, after reading "Little Red Riding Hood," ask your child how Little Red Riding Hood felt, how the wolf felt, how the carpenter felt, how Grandmother felt at different points in the story. You may want to point out that it is fun in the short run to hate bad guys, but in the long run it pays to learn that bad guys have feelings (e.g., Wolf was hungry and was just trying to stay alive) and that there are few, if any, bad guys who feel that they are bad guys.

Variation

After your child tells you a story, encourage her to imagine how the characters in the story felt. It is a very good idea to do this when some other child is presented as a dunce or a bad guy or a snob, etc.

Note

This game is designed to encourage empathy, the ability to "feel" another person's emotions, and to see different points of view. Both of these abilities have big benefits for children and parents. Children who are rated high in these abilities tend to share more with others and to take responsibility for doing things. Such children also tend to be more popular with their peers. Contrary to the view that aggressiveness will make children leaders, research shows that sharing with and otherwise helping out peers makes children leaders.

✳ 8 ✳

Early Elementary School: Seven to Nine Years

Your child now goes to school. This is a recognition that children of this age have accomplished certain basic skills and are ready for formal instruction. For example, your child should have no more pronunciation difficulties by the time he is nine. If he still has a few difficulties, he should get help from a speech pathologist at school.

Your child will have a good vocabulary, but he will continue to expand it. He may become very insistent about using words "only in the right way," a tendency that schools encourage but that stifles creativity. You can offset this tendency by playing Metaphor Games 1 and 2, Cloud Game, and You Are an Umbrella from the previous sections. Despite the fact that some children this age show some resistance to playing with words by making metaphors, most children in this age range do enjoy one of the oldest language games in the world, punning, called What's So Funny? in this section.

Along with a respect for the proper way to use words goes a somewhat exaggerated, or at least fundamentally mistaken, sense of the power of words. Your child may even believe that somehow words can magically transform things. Call something a rose and it will become a rose. Call something a frog and it will become a frog. Unfortunately, as I have pointed out previously, children also love to call each other names. The upshot of all this is that your child is likely to be troubled by some name another child has called him. If you have been playing Hurtful Words with him all along, he should have a ready response to such aggression. You may want to help him choose a response that is not itself hurtful but that will give him a way of not feeling helplessly victimized when he is called a baby or a "poopoo face" or some such childhood epithet. Perhaps he will decide to call all verbal bullies "brussel sprouts," for example.

Children who are placed in classes for the learning disabled are particularly vulnerable. In my experience, most end up being taunted as "retards" or some other equally despicable thing. It is not a good strategy to try to ignore this labeling. If you do not address this issue, your child will be left at first to wonder what the taunt meant, later to incorporate it into his self-concept. Despite the old nursery rhyme, words *do* hurt children, perhaps for a much longer time and in a much deeper way than do sticks and stones.

During this time, your child will come to understand such tricky sentences as "The doll is hard to see." Prior to this age, if you blindfolded a doll, held it right in front of your child's face, and asked him, "Is the doll hard to see?" he would have replied, "Yes." He would have misunderstood the doll as the subject of the verb "seeing." But during this time, your child will be able to figure out the sentence and reply, "Of course not!" The House That Jack Built encourages and develops his ability to understand complicated sentences.

Your child will be spending most of his efforts in learning how to read during these early elementary school years. Several of the following language games are directed toward improving skills he will use in reading. Just as language is developing long before the first word is spoken, reading has been developing long before your child is pronounced able to read. Many of the language games prior to this section have been aimed at helping your child to read. For example, researchers have found that the single largest factor in your child's success in school is how much you have read to him at home. Rhyming games and Words That Begin with *B* develop skills that are necessary for reading. Games that break down words into their parts, like Letterspeak, also contribute to a knowledge of language that makes it easier to learn to read.

Learning to read involves several stages, as characterized by a researcher in the field, Jeanne Chall. The first stage lasts for the first two grades. At this point, your child will focus on decoding words and simple stories. The second stage lasts from the second half of second grade to grade four, the end of the age group described here. During this stage, his reading will become more fluent. Your child will be skilled enough at reading individual words that he can now concentrate on understanding the meaning of a story as a whole. Encouraging your child to read familiar books facilitates the development of fluency in reading.

There is some fascinating evidence that when children are first learning to read, they may display individual differences in this learning process. Some children will seek to uphold the momentum of a story they are reading aloud, departing from the actual words in a text without stopping to correct themselves. Other children are very insistent on accuracy at the expense of momentum. Such children will correct virtually every mispronunciation and inaccurately read word, even though such corrections may become so frequent as to lose the sense of what is being read, both for child and for listener. Such children also may balk at guessing words they do not know. Both accuracy and momentum are important dimensions of the reading process, and most of these children will go on to tune in to the dimension they previously neglected. In other words, neither style should be considered preferable.

Furthermore, these reading styles seem related to more general styles of approaching the school world. Children who emphasize momentum seem more imaginative, dramatic, and integrative in their play and artwork. Sometimes they seem to be able to do more than one thing at a time. Children who emphasize accuracy seem more concerned to reproduce reality in their play and artwork, working in a concentrated, methodical, analytical fashion. They tend to do things in an orderly sequence. These styles are not to be associated with smart versus less smart children. Some very intelligent children display one style, some another. Parents and teachers should recognize that both are good alternatives and not try to turn one type of child into the other.

Children who display either of these styles seem eager to learn to read. Other children are less eager for some reason, and often reflect this by persistently gazing at the face of the adult helping them. It is as if they believe the words were written on the adult's face rather than on the page, or as if they thought the adults expected them to know what the text said without looking at it.

Your child will not change dramatically in emotions at this time. His real issues are external and social rather than internal, emotional ones. Children of this age are much more tuned into their peers than are younger children. And in every social arena of importance to his life, your child is learning The Rules. How often does every first grader hear the message, "Behave! This isn't kindergarten anymore!" Teachers will expect your child to conform to school rules with a rigor that was not displayed previously. You, his parent, will expect more conformity and responsibility from him, and you should. But other children will also impose rules on him. For example, tattling is tolerated and even encouraged by adults in preschool and kindergarten children, but your child will learn quickly that his classmates are a new political force to be reckoned with and will ostracize him if he tattles to please the grown-ups. Children make up all sorts of crazy rules for each other. When I was growing up, we were not supposed to wear green on Thursday (I forget why now), nor were we ever supposed to wear white bobby socks. The rules change from generation to generation, and that is the point—to exclude other generations, to promote greater unity by this exclusiveness. If you have not been using it, try Big Girls Don't Cry (see pp. 123–124), as it plays with all this rule-learning. In general, children develop an increased interest in games of all sorts at this time, showing great concern for the particular rules to be followed.

Another emotional issue concerns the type of rewards that are most effective in controlling your child's behavior. Prior to this time, your child would probably do anything if you promised him he could have a candy bar or play ball with you afterwards. With the cognitive limitations of young children, such rewards need to be external. But your child will work for intrinsic rewards now. He will begin to take pride in doing things right. In fact, if you use external rewards now they may backfire. Children who are paid for getting good grades may decide that the reason they are working so hard is simply for the money, not because they are interested in the material. Your child is capable of more mature thought now, and it is important that you recognize this maturity in your disciplining of him.

Piaget argues that children of this age are in the concrete operational stage of cognitive development. One of the most widely known concrete operations is conservation. Developing the ability to conserve means recognizing the irrelevance of certain perceptual changes. Put another way, younger children are susceptible to far more perceptual illusions than are adults. There are many perceptual illusions, and each has to be conquered in its own right. It may be years between such conquests. Somewhere between eight and ten years of age, your child will know that simply rolling a ball of clay into the shape of a sausage does not result in more clay. But not until he is almost twelve years of age will your child know that pouring soda from a short, wide glass to a tall, thin one does not result in more soda. These are only estimates of age. Under some circumstances, younger children can understand some types of conservation.

Regardless of the age guidelines, the ability to conserve is an important milestone in development. It is related to abstractness of thinking. Compared to younger sensorimotor and preoperational children, concrete observational children are capable of more abstraction and are less utterly dependent on the physical world around them for their thinking. Nonetheless, concrete operational children have their limits, which will become apparent when we discuss the onset of formal operations in the next section.

The most important games in this section are What's So Funny? and Tell It in Your Own Words. A number of games (Which Is a Picture of Communication?, A Great Big Mean Slimy Running Yellow Moon, Letterspeak, and Back Writing) focus on helping your child to write, the skill that becomes the primary emphasis of the last section of games in this book.

THING IN A BOX

Purpose

To encourage your child to pay careful attention to how he speaks.

Props

A box and any available object.

Game

Put an object into a box without letting your child see what you are doing. Tell him to guess what is in the box. Let him ask as many questions as he wants, so long as they can be answered with a simple yes or no. Have him rephrase any question that cannot be answered with yes or no into a permissible form. Encourage him to shift from simply naming things that could possibly be in the box to asking things *about* the object, such as whether it is red or round or whether it makes a noise or not.

Variations

1. Play this game with an inexpensive prize in the box and a group of children at a party. The person who guesses the object first, of course, gets to keep it.

2. Again at a party, divide the children into teams of three or four. Have them discuss strategies for asking questions. Put a set of inexpensive prizes in the box, and the team that guesses the

type of object gets one prize each. This variation encourages co-operation as well as competition.

WHICH IS A PICTURE OF COMMUNICATION?

Purpose

To see which words your child understands, to encourage an understanding of new words, and to help your child be comfortable in a standard testing situation.

Game

Take any group of pictures, such as those you would find in comic strips, and think of a word that only one picture depicts. Ask your child which picture shows "communication" (two people talking) or "dilapidation" (a house that is falling apart) or "frustration" (a dog pulling on a rope trying, but failing, to reach a cat who is walking nearby) or "deluge" (Garfield pouring a bucket of water over his head) and so forth. Ask him why he chose that picture and respond appropriately. The types of words you choose should change as your child grows older and more verbal. Use words from stories you have read to your child at bedtime and explained to him then.

Variation

Give your child a word and ask him to draw a picture depicting it. Ask him to explain it and respond appropriately.

WHAT IS A LUMKI?

Purpose

To encourage your child to figure out the meanings of words from their context.

Props

For Variation 1, you need books that your child mostly understands but which include unknown words. Classics such as *Alice
in Wonderland, Tom Sawyer,* and *Wind in the Willows* are likely
candidates for this age. A dictionary such as *Webster's Ninth New
Collegiate* also would be useful.

Game

Read the following sentences to your child and ask him to figure
out the meanings of the italicized nonsense words. Nonsense
words are used in this version because your child cannot have
encountered them before and therefore is forced to rely totally on
context for defining them. If he enjoys this game, make up new
nonsense words. I think you will find that making up words is a
language game that is fun for adults.

- The *luppiluppi* sang sweetly in the tree.
- A carpenter used a *raxin* to smooth the wood.
- The *snorgish* man shook his fist at his wife when she
  sneezed, beat his dog while it slept, and broke down the
  front door when it wouldn't open—all because it was an-
  other rainy day.
- The princess put her handkerchief in a beautiful silk *lumbi.*
- Elves sometimes *bishle* you when you are asleep and make
  you dream about candy and ice cream and toys.
- Cindy ran carefully and *meggly* to avoid all the garbage in
  the city street.
- The *oshkilostra* grew beside the railroad tracks.
- Mark did not want to go to school today, *espergras* he had
  a test in his worst subject, geography.
- Emily's grandmother always served her a hot cup of *framoshka* when she came to visit. She later found out that
  framoshka was good for curing headaches.

- To join the secret club, you have to learn how to give the secret *snibble* with your hands.
- Don't ever *looba* your clay or you won't be able to shape it into new things.
- The new girl was so pretty and so smart and so kind and so *partrekich* that none of the boys could think of anything to say to her even though they all liked her.
- An *isiola* came out of its cave at night and began to hunt for mice to eat.

Variations

1. When your child asks you what a word means while you are reading him a book, ask him to guess its meaning. Repeat the word in its context. You even may want to encourage him to begin to use a dictionary to check his guesses.

2. If your child is not ready for any of these versions, watch the "Smurfs" Saturday morning cartoon. The characters substitute "smurf" for a number of different words that your child clearly knows. Ask him what it means in a number of different settings.

Note

A child's early definitions of words are primarily concrete descriptions of what something does or what it looks like. With age and practice, children eventually define things in terms of synonyms and membership in larger categories (a buffalo is defined as "an animal," for example).

The ability to define words from context is a cornerstone of reading and is one reason that extensive reading is more likely to develop a child's vocabulary than is extensive drill on definitions of words. This game points out to a child that he has this ability and encourages him to practice it.

WHAT'S SO FUNNY?

Purpose

To develop your child's sense of humor by highlighting the double meanings of words.

Game

Children ages six to eight increasingly enjoy puns like the following:

- "Order, order in the court!" "A ham and cheese on rye, your honor."
- Why did the boy throw the clock out the window? He wanted to make time fly.
- Why did the girl get rid of a penny? She didn't like the scent.
- What is black and white and re(a)d all over? A newspaper.
- When does a school have no desks? When it is a school of fish.
- When is a rose not a rose? When it is rows of teeth.
- Why is a telephone rich? Because it makes a lot of rings.
- What did the big frying pan call the little frying pan? Small fry.
- Why is bread lazy? Because it just loafs around.
- Why did the lion buy an expensive new suit? Because he was a dandelion.

Variation

With a little practice, you can create your own puns for your child. Say something like, "If you don't sit down, I'll wring your neck," and make a pulling motion near his neck, saying "RRRinnggg, rrriinnnggg." Or, "I have a run in my stockings. Bet you can't catch it."

A GREAT BIG MEAN SLIMY RUNNING
YELLOW MOON

Purpose

To focus your child's attention on adjectives and to create imaginary characters.

Game

Choose some object and give it a one-word description. Ask your child to add another one-word description and combine the two. Take turns back and forth. For example, you might say, "I'm thinking of a shoe. You know what kind of a shoe it is? It is a big shoe. What else is it?"

"A smelly shoe."

"Okay, it is a smelly big shoe. I think it is also an ornery shoe, an ornery smelly big shoe. What kind of a shoe is it?"

"A sniffy shoe."

"That's a good one. A sniffy ornery smelly big shoe. What else?"

"A swinging sniffy ornery smelly big shoe. What else?" And so on.

Variation

Instead of your repeating all the adjectives in order, have your child do it when it is his turn. The first person to give the wrong order gets tickled. For example, you begin by saying, "I'm thinking of a frog, a nasty frog. What else is he?"

Your child replies, "He is a sneaky nasty frog."

You reply, "He is a bog-dwelling sneaky nasty frog."

Your child replies, "He is a bony bog-dwelling sneaky nasty frog."

You reply, "He is a nighttime bony bog-dwelling sneaky nasty frog."

Your child says, "He is a yucky-green nighttime bony bog-dwelling sneaky nasty frog."

You say, "He is a red-eyed yucky-green nighttime bog-dwelling sneaky nasty frog." (You forget to say "bony.")

Your child catches your omission and tickles you, but a wonderful character just has been invented.

THE HOUSE THAT JACK BUILT

Purpose

To improve your child's understanding of complex sentences.

Game

Use the following sentences for starters and then make up your own:

- The cow that the man is holding is sleepy. Who is sleepy?
- The man who is wearing the red hat is standing by the little boy. Who is wearing the red hat?
- The rabbit that the man was chasing was fast. Who was fast?
- The book that is resting on the old table is dusty. What is old?
- The cat with the red boots who climbed the tall mountain is talking to the old duck in the yellow raincoat. Who climbed the mountain? Who was wearing a raincoat? What was tall? What was old?

Variation

Read "The House That Jack Built" and ask questions about it. In case you don't have it on hand, here is the most complex sentence in that classic:

This is the farmer sowing the corn
that kept the cock that crowed in the morn
that waked the priest all shaven and shorn
that married the man all tattered and torn
that kissed the maiden all forlorn
that milked the cow with the crumpled horn
that tossed the dog
that worried the cat
that killed the rat
that ate the malt
that lay in the house that Jack built.

You could draw pictures of the characters yourself and ask your child who tossed the dog or who waked the priest or who was forlorn or a number of other things.

TELL IT IN YOUR OWN WORDS

Purpose

To give your child practice in reproducing the gist of stories.

Props

Several new stories, relatively short and simple.

Game

Read a new story to your child, then send in your spouse or a grandparent and have your child tell him or her the story in his own words.

Variations

1. Get a group of people, read a story to your child in a whisper, have him tell it to the next person in a whisper, have that

person tell it to the next, and so forth around the group. Have the last person tell the story aloud. Read the original story aloud and compare the two versions. It is bound to be a funny comparison.

2. Have your child retell a story that is very familiar to him, such as "The Three Bears" or "The Three Pigs," to a much younger child. Compliment him if he simplifies the story so that the younger child can understand it and if he keeps calling the younger child's attention back to the task at hand.

LETTERSPEAK

Purpose

To make a game of spelling skills.

Game

Make up a special language that consists of segmenting each word into its component sounds when you speak. Silent letters do not count. Simply ask your child to sound out some request in order to get the hang of this "secret code." "Can I go outside?" becomes "Ka ah en I go oh ow tah ss I da?" You reply, "yeh eh ss." And so forth.

Variations

1. For a short time, require that you and your child communicate only by saying the sounds of each letter, including silent letters, of each word you want to say to each other. "May I have some milk?" becomes "Em ay wy I ha ah va eh ss oo em eh em I el kah?" You reply, "Oh en el wy I eff wy oo u ss ay wy pah el ee ay ess ee." Your child has to say, "Pah el ee ay ess ee." You say,

"oh kay." This variation will work only with older children, who know how to spell a number of words.

2. A famous version of this spelling game is pig latin. For those of you who have forgotten how to play, it goes like this: Transpose the first letter of a word to the end of the word and add "ay," pronounced like "hay." Some words like "a," "an," and "the," and words beginning with vowels can be left alone. For example, if you want to say, "Molly took back the book," the pig latin version would be, "Olly-may ook-tay ack-bay the ook-bay." It takes a little practice to do this even for parents, but children love to do it.

Note

About one in three children will find this game difficult at the end of first grade, so you may want to keep turns especially short, aiming for sounding out or spelling single words at a time. In any case, keep this a game, with the focus on fun rather than instruction. Of course, instruction will result, but this will be more likely if the child does not worry about anything except communicating true to the "secret code."

BACK WRITING

Purpose

To make a game of spelling.

Game

Have your child spell out a word on your back and see if you can guess it. If he misspells it, deliberately (mis)pronounce it the way he spelled it and have him try again. This is a good game to make of words he is supposed to learn how to spell, but it is also a good way to pass the time in waiting rooms.

Variations

1. To encourage reading skills, switch roles. You spell out challenging words on your child's back and have him guess them.

2. If you have more than one school-aged child, have them play this game with each other.

3. Spell out messages for each other.

Note

This game comes from a friend of mine who is a teacher, Molly Rosencranz. Her second-grade class enjoys it, so it easily could be turned into a party game.

SIGNS

Purpose

To show your child the many uses of language by not letting him speak for a while; also to show your child how sign language works.

Props

A sign language dictionary is useful for the variation.

Game

Tell your child that you are having a No Talking Time. Tell him that for the next hour you both can talk only by gesturing to each other, but you can gesture as much as you want.

Variations

1. Remember some signs you invent for things. After your No Talking Time is up, compare your signs with American Sign Language (Ameslan).

2. Learn some standard Ameslan signs. Have an Ameslan-Only Time, such as dinner.

Note

This game is a good way to get a group of overly noisy children to quiet down without yelling at them. Although this is billed as a No Talking Time to highlight its main rule, it can turn into a very active, though quiet, talking time because, after all, signing *is* talking. Until recently, sign language often was accused of not being a real language. But extensive recent research has contradicted that old prejudice. Deaf children no longer have their hands figuratively tied so that they will not become "dependent" on signing, as oralist methods of teaching the deaf used to do. Instead, deaf children now usually are taught sign language. One of *Sesame Street*'s many virtues is that it teaches some signs to all children who watch it. Many people have discovered that sign language is fun as well as of vital importance to deaf individuals.

This is also a good game to play with your child whenever either one of you has a sore throat.

✳ 9 ✳

Late Elementary School: Nine to Eleven Years and Up

This book was written to facilitate communication between you and your child. However, in encouraging your child to communicate well with you, you also encourage her ability to communicate with others, including her peers. Lowry Hemphill and her colleagues discovered that fourth-, fifth-, and sixth-grade children are quite sensitive to other children's ability to communicate. They took videotapes of children talking to other children and edited the tapes so that certain children either appeared to converse fluently or else made lengthy pauses, switched topics of conversation frequently, and repeated things they previously said. Other children observed the tapes and were told that the taped children "needed special help for math, reading, language, and social studies" (the current language for describing mental retardation). Children described the "fluent" children in more positive terms than those same children when they were depicted as conversing poorly. A child who can talk well to her peers, initiating and sustaining topics of conversation and avoiding lengthy pauses, is a child likely to be accepted by them.

Writing is the final language skill to be developed, and most of your child's language-learning efforts during this time will be directed to this end. In this final chapter I have some games that will help your child work on writing skills while talking to you. Even though many good speakers are not good writers, the gulf between writing and speaking is not as large as it might first seem.

How does writing develop? The process is so complex that it has not been as thoroughly studied as have other aspects of language. We do know a few points of interest. In the fourth grade, your child typically will show a concern for her audience for the first time. She will worry about how her teacher, grandparent, or friend will respond to what she writes. Initially, this will slow your child's writing, making the task much more difficult for her. But this concern with her audience will also prompt her to revise her writing, which she probably firmly resisted before. Of course, revision and a good estimation of one's audience are essential aspects of good writing.

At first, your child will write sentences that are much simpler than the ones she speaks. But by the end of elementary school, this will reverse: she will write much more complex sentences than the ones she speaks.

Writing involves the development of numerous technical details, the discussion of which is beyond the scope of this book. Suffice it to say that children take a long time to master these details and even longer to be creative beyond that.

Your child will have a good sense of how to tell and write a narrative at this time. She will move on to learn other types of writing. At this age, your child will spend a great deal of time and effort in school learning how to write reports. She will learn to organize information more effectively, as well as to use different tenses. Children generally have a more difficult time learning to write reports, as opposed to stories. One reason for this may be because stories are frequently read and told at home, while reports seldom are. I have included a game called Reports that encourages oral exchanges of such information.

What can you do to help your child improve her writing? First as with her earlier language skills, do not correct her writing too much. Limit yourself to one suggestion for improvement per effort, unless she asks you specifically for more. Children want to learn to write correctly, but they need to feel that it is a manageable task and one that will be rewarded by the enjoyment of their audience.

Second, ask your child to write daily. Ask her to write a letter to Grandma one day, a story for Valentine's Day another. Buy her a diary, and encourage her to record the most important thing that happens to her every day. If your son resists a "sissy diary," buy him a notebook and ask him to keep a "journal" like most great writers have done, recording what happens and what he thinks about during each day.

Good writing is good thinking. Improvement in one improves the other. Reasons is a game that works on clarifying thinking, which will in turn clarify writing.

Encourage your child to read her own writing aloud, as in Poetry Aloud.

Encourage your child to read novels and poetry. Reading good writing improves every aspect of writing. Jeanne Chall's description of the several stages of reading development characterizes the third stage (grades four through eight) as one in which children read to learn new information. Talk to your child about poems or novels you both have read. If you do not remember these, reread them either before or after your child reads them to allow for such discussion. The fourth stage (high school) is characterized by your child's increased ability to draw inferences and understand different points of view. Continue reading and discussing the same works. Your child will undoubtedly surprise you with her perspective on the material. Some older high school students and college-age individuals are capable of true criticism of what they read. You should encourage your child to criticize material, even though you may find her lacerating one of your favorite novels. Remember, criticism is a valuable skill. Go ahead and point out why you disagree with her, but make it clear that you are proud of her for being critical.

An increased vocabulary improves writing. Your child may acquire over five thousand new words between the ages of nine and eleven. The best ways of improving vocabulary are through reading and recognizing the relationships between words, something that the game of Stems is aimed at doing.

Large individual differences in writing ability emerge during this time. Some children become experts in spelling but lag behind others in their ability to produce good metaphors, for example. In general, developmental differences in language, cognition, and emotions are much more difficult to articulate, let alone tie to some particular age, as children grow older. This is because your child will express her individuality in virtually everything she does. Put another way, children begin to seem far more different from other same-aged children than they did early on in life, although, as we have seen, there are individual differences at birth. Two ten-month-old infants have a lot more in common than two ten-year-olds do.

In terms of cognitive development, one important issue is that of memory. Your child will be using her memory extensively in her schoolwork now, memorizing multiplication tables, geographical facts, etc. There are some ways in which you can help her to improve her memory. By ten or eleven years of age, most children organize information they are asked to study. But not all children do. Nor do all children organize information equally well. You could work with your child to help her do this more effectively. Have her outline a textbook chapter, for example.

Another way of improving memory is by elaborating information to be learned. Talk with your child about what she is studying. Chances are you will relearn some information yourself. In any case, such discussions will make the material more memorable to her. For example, if you tell her a story about seeing the steel mills in Pittsburgh dump fiery slag at night when you visited there, she will have no problem remembering that Pittsburgh was once a premier producer of steel.

If you have no anecdote to provide, and your child is having a hard time remembering that, for example, Richmond is the capital of Virginia, you might recommend that she resort to forming an image linking Richmond with Virginia. Tell her to imagine her friend Virginia sitting on a mound of money—Virginia on a Rich Mound. Even better, have her come up with such images herself.

This age range sees the onset of the final stage of cognitive development, at least as articulated by Jean Piaget. This is the time when your child will enter the stage of formal operations. She will begin to become systematic in her thinking, considering a variety of possible alternative explanations of some event, instead of simply settling on the first one that comes to mind. She will become capable of thinking things out in a logical way. She will be able to consider hypothetical situations. She can even begin to consider a situation from a point of view that she dislikes. In fact, she should be encouraged to do so.

With this cognitive advancement, your child will mature in her moral reasoning. There is considerable debate about whether girls mature in the same way that boys mature in terms of their moral reasoning. Lawrence Kohlberg studied boys ages seven to sixteen. He found that the younger children resolved moral dilemmas by considering the likely consequences of alternative responses, or, in other words, the effect of responses on other people. These boys sought to avoid punishment and gain rewards. After age ten, boys are as tuned into rules and laws as they are the consequences of responses. Occasionally, in their later teens, boys show a tendency to reason beyond laws and conventional moral prescriptions for behavior. Some of the time, at least some young men tend to develop a belief that if individual rights are violated by certain laws, then the laws themselves should be broken and even changed. At the highest possible level, young men may articulate their own moral beliefs and resolve dilemmas in terms of this individual perspective on justice, but preserve the rights of others in the process. Girls may show a continued preoccupation with the needs of others and with the effect of a person's actions upon other people. Carol Gilligan has pointed out that this divergent path of moral development in girls deserves equal consideration to that of boys.

Whether or not there are sex differences in moral development, your child will develop her moral reasoning during this time. You may assist your child in this endeavor by talking frankly about moral issues: war, religion, abortion, mercy killing. Beware of being overly critical of her opinions. Remember that she is in the process of sorting things out. Genuine respect for and concern for her opinions is invaluable for her moral development.

Most games in this chapter are designed for fun as well as to facilitate writing skills either directly or indirectly. Turn About and Lump Was Here Again Today stimulate communication. I hope these games will amuse you and your child and keep your conversation flowing. Unfortunately, some children during this age range sink into a sullen silence towards their parents, although by the age of twelve they are capable of talking almost like adults to adults. Never let such silence continue. Ask your child what the matter is, and if she continues to refuse to discuss the matter with you, seek outside help.

DESCRIBE IT

Purpose

To encourage observational skills by encouraging verbal ones.

Props

Paper, pencils, and any interesting object. I recommend flowers, an old pair of shoes, a rock, or a butterfly.

Game

Set an object between you and your child. In ten minutes, write down descriptions of the object in as many ways as you can think of. When the time is up, compare. See who has the most descriptive comments. See how many things you observed in common. See who has the most imaginative descriptions.

Variations

1. Play this game at a birthday party with a large group of children. Limit the time to five minutes. Have everyone read their list aloud. Offer prizes for (a) the person with the most descriptive comments, (b) the person with the most objective comments (e.g., it is 3⅛ inches long), (c) the person with the most poetic comments (e.g., it is the color of a yellow traffic sign on a rainy day), and (d) the best detective (e.g., the person who guesses what kind of individual owns the pair of shoes).

2. Another good party game is to arrange for a friend to knock on the door and deliver something like a surprise pizza. After everyone has finished their pizza, surprise them with the game of describing the delivery person. (Only polite descriptions are allowed.) After everyone has finished their descriptions, bring in the delivery person. Give first prize to the person who wrote the most accurate comments and a booby prize to the person whose description was the most far out.

Note

This game is based on one of the few exercises used by both scientists and creative writing professors. There are very few jobs that do not require a keen sense of observation, and both scientific and poetic observation require a sensitivity to language that can and should be developed. You can begin to play this game now, but do not stop playing it when your child is nine. If your child goes to college, chances are she will play this game in at least a couple of classes. It is instructive, as well as fun, for adults and children.

LUMP WAS HERE AGAIN TODAY

Purpose

To communicate with your child about difficult feelings in a humorous way.

Game

Invent a character. Name him. Introduce him to your child and tell some stories about him. Do this on repeated occasions. The more you talk about him, the more colorful a character he will become. For example, you might introduce Lump, a fellow who has the best of intentions but always gets in your way when you are trying to make a good impression or succeed at work. Lump is not very good-looking. He makes stupid jokes. He spills coffee on his boss's shirt (the day you actually did this). Yesterday he wore his shirt the whole day with the tag hanging outside the neck and typed a report so poorly that it probably will get rejected just because it looks so messy. He called his father-in-law a toad, and his father-in-law overheard him. The worst part is that Lump knows he is a jerk. But the more he says, "I am a jerk," the worse he does. And so forth. Ask your child if she ever gets visits from Lump. Encourage her to tell you about them.

Variation

Encourage your child to invent a character of her own.

IMAGINARY RECIPES

Purpose

To stimulate conversation on difficult or emotional topics.

Game

With your child, compose imaginary recipes for the following things: love, hatred, happiness, sadness, friends, hope, success, failure, anger, marriage, divorce, father, mother, being a star, winning.

A recipe for love might begin by your child saying, "First you have to go to the movies and meet somebody next to you." You say, "Then you have to look that person directly in the eyes for a little bit without blinking." Your child might say, "Then you have to buy the person popcorn." And so it could go.

Variation

Play up the recipe angle of this conversational game by devising recipes for "Love Soup," "Gloomy Cucumbers," "Tomato Hate," and so on. What kind of food would go into "Love Soup," for example?

GIBBERISH

Purpose

Having fun with language.

Props

Typewriter.

Game

As any typist knows, a good way to generate gibberish is to move one hand on the keyboard over one letter. Put your right index finger on the *h* instead of the *j* and type anything. Copy from a magazine article, if you cannot think of a thing to say. The results will be close enough to English to be pronounceable but very funny. The game is to have your child read this gibberish aloud.

If you cannot type, just close your eyes and hunt-and-punch a lot of "words." Your child may want to do this sort of typing herself.

Variations

1. After both of you have typed and read a lot of gibberish, try just verbalizing gibberish, making it up as you go. Act out things you are trying to say. Ham it up. You may find yourselves fixing on a couple of favorite words, which will become your secret code with each other.

2. See What Is a Lumki? (pp. 195–197) and have your child try to figure out what each word in a typed sentence of gibberish might mean, as well as the sentence as a whole.

Note

I suppose I could have said that Variation 2 points out the fact that there is more to communicating with language than just the words exchanged. Tone, manner of speaking (loud, soft, harsh, polite—try them all), facial and body expression—all contribute to communication. But really I think this is stretching things a bit. It's just fun to speak gibberish on occasion.

LOONG TIME, SHORT TIM

Purpose

To teach your child about the relationship between spelling and pronunciation, focusing on long and short vowels.

Game

Develop a new sort of pig latin game by deciding to pronounce all words in a conversation for a while with long vowel sounds. This will take time and practice for adults but is amusing. For example, you might say, "We weel go foor ay ridee ine thee care, okay? Whate do yohooo thigh-nk of thate?" Your child must reply, "Greeate, I have (rhymes with cave) -ee to geet so-mee breeade." And so forth. All vowels in a word (silent or not) have to be pronounced and pronounced as long vowels. That is all you have to do.

Variation

Try the same thing, only this time all vowels must be pronounced as short vowels. For example, "I (as in Tim) duh not fell lick having weh-in-ers for dinner tuhnit, what duh yuh think?" Your child might reply, "I wo-(as in not)ud lick pi(as in "in")-zza and Pep-sih." And so forth. See who can keep it up the longest and the best.

WHAT IS A PROMISE?

Purpose

To develop your child's ability to define words and to learn new ones.

Props

A dictionary such as *Webster's Ninth New Collegiate Dictionary.*

Game

Use any word your child knows and take turns trying to define it as closely as possible to the dictionary definition. For example, use the word "communication." Your child, who always goes first in this game, says that "it is like when two people are talking to each other." You say that it is when two people talk to each other and understand each other. The dictionary defines it as "an act or instance of transmitting . . . an exchange of information . . . a process by which meanings are exchanged between individuals through a common system of symbols." Since the dictionary does not emphasize understanding, you judge that your child won this round. Some good words to try to define include "nice," "bad,"

Chapter 9

"mortgage," "marriage," "trampoline," "word," "sentence," "story," "friend," "love," "hate," "happy."

Variations

1. Open the dictionary to any page and pick out the weirdest word, making sure that it is one you don't know. Have everyone in your family write out a definition for the word. When you have all done so, compare your definitions with each other first and then with the real definition. For example, suppose you opened the dictionary and found the word "chalcid." Your child says that it probably means it tastes like onions, while your spouse says that it means chalky, and you say that it probably means challenging. It is really a type of insect.

2. A more advanced version of this game can be played with older children and adults. Have one person select an unusual word in the dictionary. Have all the other players write down on a piece of paper what they think the definition of the word is. Have everyone read their definition aloud. Then vote on who is closest to the true definition. The person whose definition receives the most votes gets one point. Read the true definition of the word. The person who correctly guessed the true definition gets a point. Play until someone scores twenty-five points (or some other agreed-upon total).

CATEGORIES

Purpose

To encourage your child to think of things in larger groups.

Game

Say, "First one who can't think of a fruit gets tickled by the other one. Banana." Your child should name some other fruit such as apples. You name cherries. Your child adds blueberries. And so forth. The first person who cannot name another fruit gets tickled by the other person. If your child names something that is not a fruit, like apple pie, or something that has been named before, say that it does not count and that she should try again.

Try a number of different categories, including animals, furniture, clothes, body parts, colors, shapes, flowers, insects, plants, toys, appliances, holidays.

Variation

Have your child name all the members of a category that she can name in a minute. Keep a record and see if she can beat her own previous record.

STEMS

Purpose

To show the connections between words.

Props

A dictionary is useful for extending the game.

Game

Using a word stem, take turns with your child thinking of words that include that stem. Examples are "man," "mar," "mem." There are so many stems that it is far more sensible for me to steer you to a dictionary than to list more of them. Glance at a dictionary. Check the guide words at the top of the page. When you find two or more guide words that begin with the same several letters, you have a good stem. Proper names and geographical names are okay, as long as they are standard ones. The last person who can think of a word with the stem gets to finish the ice cream.

Variations

1. You can use this game to review prefixes such as "pre," "re," "pro," "in," or "dis." Consult your dictionary to make sure that words named are permissible. Teachers might find this a good way to teach prefixes, letting every child in the class take a turn naming a word that begins with a certain prefix. This game also works well with suffixes such as "tion" or "ly."

2. With either the main game or Variation 1, you may want to have both you and your child list independently as many words as possible that include the stem or prefix. Whoever lists the most words wins.

Note

Teaching your child the relationship between words, as this game is designed to do, is a far more effective way of building vocabulary than drilling her on specific words.

TREASURE HUNT

Purpose

To give your child practice in giving directions and in taking them.

Game

On your spouse's birthday or the appropriate Parent Day, have your child hide a present, make up a set of directions for finding it, and write these down, one at a time, each on a separate slip of paper. Hide the clues in the appropriate places. For example, the first clue might be to go upstairs and take three steps to the left.

Upstairs, three steps to the left, your spouse might find another clue that directed him or her to "turn around all the way and go down the hall fifty-five steps, turn right, and bend down." Having done that, your spouse would find a third clue, and so forth.

Variation

Switch roles and arrange a treasure hunt for your child. Give clues appropriate for your child's reading level.

SYNONYMS

Purpose

To play with the similarities between words.

Props

A thesaurus.

Game

Using any word you wish, take turns coming up with words that mean almost the same thing. Whoever is the last person to think of a word gets to eat a cookie or some other treat. Good words to start with include "good," "bad," "nice," "old," "crazy," "rude," "vain," "small," "large," "forget," "evidence," "trust," "intelligent," "quiet," "smelly," "delicious," "grave," "body," "die," "kill," "sea," "light," "shine," "freeze," "leave," "vagrant," "speed up," "network," "everywhere," "involve," "influence," "trash," "strong," "end," "begin," "baby," "past," "strange," "spread," "think," "always," "love." Consult a thesaurus to see which words have a long list of synonyms after them because such words make good, long-running candidates for this game. Close the thesaurus without looking at specific synonyms, or if you cannot do that, choose a list of good candidates for the next time you play the game, when you will have forgotten specific entries.

Rules: (a) Decide on a part of speech beforehand and stick to it. For example, "trash" could be played as a noun or verb but not both in one game. (b) Slang terms and expressions consisting of more than one word are permitted and encouraged. (c) Specific examples are not permitted in this game. Naming types of animals instead of synonyms for "animal" is playing Categories, not Synonyms. (d) Challenges are permitted, and the thesaurus (or dictionary) should be used to decide who is right. If the challenger is right, she wins. If she is not, she loses. Start another word at that point.

Variations

1. List all the synonyms you and your child think of. Compare your list to the list in the thesaurus and see how well you both have done.

2. For more advanced players, you could try coming up with synonyms and then saying how each synonym is different from the original word.

PARAPHRASE

Purpose

To encourage skill in paraphrasing, which in turn is useful for good writing and general sensitivity to language.

Game

Using any sentence, take turns with your child paraphrasing it. Point out inevitable differences between the paraphrases and the original sentence. Sentences on billboards make good material for turning this into a car game. For example, change "Reach for the exceptional" into "Reach for exceptional things," or "Reach for things that are exceptional," or "Reach for outstanding things," or "Reach for the outstanding," or "Reach for the superb" or "You should reach for the exceptional," or "The exceptional should be reached for by you." I could go on and on, combining these suggested alterations in various ways.

Variations

1. Set specific goals. For example, ask your child to see if she can say the same thing three different ways. Try four next time, then five, and so on. Sentences can be rewritten as many as fifteen different ways (by skilled adults). Always discuss differences between paraphrases and the original after you are done. Pick the most poetic, or the most scientific, or the most boring versions. See which version is closest to the original.

2. Take any written sentence. Both you and your child should try to paraphrase the sentence as many ways as possible. The winner gets to make popcorn or a snack of her choice.

3. See if your child can improve on sentences written by famous authors.

Note

It is a much debated question in some linguistic circles about whether true paraphrase is ever really possible. You can conduct this debate with your child by keeping up a running search for two different ways of saying exactly the same thing. Of course, I do not believe you ever will find two ways of saying *exactly* the same thing. Instead, whenever you see the similarities between two statements, you also will soon notice the differences between them. And that is really the point of this game. Engaging in the game of Paraphrase will improve even an adult's sensitivity to language. It is also fun.

PARTS OF SPEECH

Purpose

To show connections between words.

Props

You may want to use paper and pencil for this.

Game

Give your child a word and see how many different parts of speech it can be turned into. For example:

	Red	Bright	Give
Noun	redness	brightness	gift, given, giver
Verb	redden	brighten, brightening	give
Adjective	red, redder, reddest	bright, brighter, brightest	given
Adverb	redly	brightly	—

Preposition, pronoun, and interjection forms usually are not possible.

Be sure to generate what possible parts of speech would be even if you do not believe they are permissible. When you have generated these forms, consult the dictionary to see which are acceptable. Did you know, for example, that "redly" was permissible?

Variation

Play this game with your child and see who comes up with the most permissible forms. Also, see who comes up with the funniest invented forms.

Note

Encouraging your child to see the connections between words, as this game is designed to do, is a better way of improving vocabulary than drilling her on the specific meanings of words. This is another game you will never really outgrow. Advertisers make a lot of money turning words into hybrid parts of speech, a practice that makes self-appointed guardians of the language apoplectic.

THE RAIN STAYS MAINLY ON THE PLAIN

Purpose

To heighten your child's awareness of the poetic device of assonance, in which words share a prominent internal sound.

Game

Take turns trying to develop as long a sentence as you can of words that have identical or similar internal vowel sounds. For example, you might say, "Only phony ponies joke." Your child might reply, "Pale gray rain." The winner is the person who comes up with the most assonant words in one more-or-less sensible sentence or phrase. Each phrase may take a while to produce, so this might be a game for a long car ride or a game that runs for several days.

Variations

1. Instead of playing for long sequences of assonant words, play for the most beautiful assonant sentence.

2. Since playing this game will make you and your child more sensitive to assonance, be on the lookout for long, beautiful assonant sequences in poems and prose. Form a mutual collection of these.

WONDERFUL WILLOWY WORDS

Purpose

To draw your child's attention to the poetic device of alliteration, in which a string of words begin with the same letter.

Game

Take turns with your child composing aloud sentences made up entirely of words that begin with one sound or group of sounds. For example, you might say "Alice arrested an army attendant," or "Three threatening thrushes thrashed through thread." Your child might say "Growling grinches" or "Big Bob beats bananas."

Variations

1. Work your way through the alphabet. You make up a sentence of *A* words, and your child makes up a sentence of *B* words, and so forth.

2. Pick any beginning sound you like. Play the game for a point per word. You would get five points for the "Alice arrested" sentence, six for the "Three threatening thrushes" sentence above. Take turns with your child. See who has the most points in ten turns. See who can score the most points in one turn.

3. See who can make up the silliest sentence.

4. See who can make up the most poetic sentence.

METAPHOR GAME 3

Purpose

To encourage creativity with language.

Game

Put the names of at least a dozen common (unrelated) objects into a hat and draw out two at a time. Take turns figuring out how the

two could be related. Try different words each time, but for starters you might try the following: "ice," "book," "dog," "tomato,"
"boy," "girl," "love," "eyes," "daisy," "kite," "hammer," "car."
Sometimes the most unlikely pairs of words can stimulate the
most original metaphor. This game works better as a writing
exercise. For example, your teenager might come up with the
following: "Joe was a strong man. When he tossed his *hammer*
away in disgust, it flew out of the construction site like a *kite* in a
March wind. He never did find it."

Variation

Read a Shakespearean play (or some other work of good fiction)
aloud and notice some of the metaphors in the passages you read.
Talk about whether the two objects being compared would have
struck you as similar *before* Shakespeare made them seem so in the
context of his writing. Talk about why, for example, he had Romeo
exclaim that "Juliet is the sun!" Point out the network of images of
light and dark that you find throughout the play, and show how
often love systematically is compared to illumination. Juliet later
exclaims, "Come, night; come, Romeo; come, thou day in night" to
mention one of many other such references.

POETRY ALOUD

Purpose

To encourage your child to hear what she reads (and writes).

Props

A poetry anthology and a tape recorder.

Game

Take turns with your child reading poems aloud.

Variations

1. Tape-record your readings, unless your child is overly self-conscious, in which case you may cause her to stammer.
2. Have your child tape-record poems or stories she has written and play them back to her. These recordings may make good presents for grandparents who live a great distance away.

Note

Variation 2 is one of my favorite ways of trying to improve students' writing on the college level. I truly believe that people would not write as awkwardly as they often do if they read more of their writing aloud or at least figuratively could hear what they wrote. So this is a game for adults, as well as for children.

LIKE ROBERT FROST

Purpose

To help your child become sensitive to styles of writing.

Props

An anthology of poetry that contains several works by each of a number of poets. The variation calls for novels by several authors.

Game

Have your child read several poems by one poet and then write a poem herself in the style of that poet. Good candidates to begin with include Robert Frost, Walt Whitman, Emily Dickinson, and William Carlos Williams. Be sure to appreciate whatever your child writes, pointing out what things she has imitated well. This is a good game for a rainy day or when your child is sick.

Variation

After your child has read a novel, have her write a short story in the style of that author. Jane Austen, Ernest Hemingway, Mark Twain, Charlotte or Emily Brontë, Henry James, Charles Dickens, and Thomas Hardy are good candidates for this exercise, since they all have clear, well-developed styles of writing.

Note

This exercise may seem too advanced for elementary school children, but there is good evidence that they are quite capable of being sensitive to literary style and of imitating it. This game is one that can be started early and never outgrown.

REASONS

Purpose

To help your child develop reasoning.

Props

You need a picture to play the first game. You can draw an appropriate one yourself, such as one of three people of different heights whom you name. You might even want to draw pictures of people your child knows. For Variation 5, you need a puppet that you dub as a silly puppet. A clown puppet works wonderfully.

Game

After you have drawn the pictures and named them, tell your child that Jimmy is taller than Susie, but Susie is taller than Elmo, and ask your child who is tallest. Do the same for older, happier, prettier, funnier, etc.

You can draw different pictures each time, or you can add different features, one at a time. In the latter case, you may end up with a drawing of the tallest (body), oldest (hair color), happiest (mouth), prettiest (eyes), funniest (hat) woman clown, a drawing of the shortest, youngest, least happy, least pretty, least funny woman clown, and a drawing reflecting middle dimensions. If your child has no problem playing this game with the pictures, then dispense with them to play the game with more challenge.

Variations

1. Syllogisms (a game for more advanced elementary school children):

Say, "All cats are animals.
　　Sam is a cat.
　　Therefore, Sam is an animal.

　　But: Just because all cats are animals,
　　and Sam is an animal,
　　it doesn't mean necessarily that Sam is a cat. He
　　could be a dog or a rabbit or a bunny or a cow."

Another example: grab a watermelon and say, "If I tell you that all melons are fruits, and this fruit that I have here is a melon, then that means that this is also a what? A fruit, right? But if I tell you that all bananas are fruits, and that what I have here is a fruit, does that mean that it is a banana?"

"If I said that all doctors are smart, and that Mr. Friebert is a doctor, it means that he is also —. But if I said that all doctors are smart, and that our friend Bill is smart, does that mean that he is a doctor? Right, it does not. Instead, he is a teacher."

Be sure to stick to real examples at first. Not until twelve can most children deal with versions of the game like the following:

"If I say that all blue people live in red houses, does that mean that all people in red houses are blue?" Elementary school children may get off track explaining that you cannot have blue people.

Note

In the field of child development, it is widely believed that only children ages eleven or twelve are capable of logical reasoning, such as is encouraged in these games. However, there is some good research indicating that as long as you use real objects to play these games, children as young as six are capable of correctly answering at least some questions requiring reasoning.

Furthermore, these games should be played at this age for instruction rather than for testing accomplishment. You should not expect your elementary school child to come up with correct answers. Instead, be delighted if she does, and if she does not, use the game as a takeoff for discussing the issues involved.

FILL IN THE BLANKS

Purpose

To point out to your child how much of written language is redundant.

Props

Two copies of a newspaper or magazine article or some other text. Passages from famous authors work well.

Game

Black out every fifth word in the passage before you. Both you and your child should try to figure out the blacked out words. When you are finished, compare your substitutions to the original text.

See which of you got the most words correct. See whether either of you improved upon the original.

Variation

Let your child play this game on her own. For the price of a photocopy, you have a good word puzzle for a rainy day.

Note

This game was adapted from something called the "cloze" method of measuring readability. The greater the number of words a person guesses correctly, the more readable that text is for her. While this technique was invented as a measure of the quality of the text rather than the reader it is fun to do this sort of guessing and it could benefit your child. This game encourages her to scan a text and predict words that she will encounter as she is reading, a skill that may help her speed up her reading while not sacrificing comprehension. After all, comprehension involves actively thinking about information you come across, something you have to do to succeed at this game.

ON THE TIP OF YOUR TONGUE

Purpose

To teach your child about how words are stored in memory.

Props

A die or penny (Variation 1) and some squares (Scrabble squares work well), each with one of the twenty-six letters of the alphabet on it.

Game

You and your child alternate turns according to the following
rules.

1. Set a time limit (set timer for thirty minutes) or a point
   limit (say one hundred points) for play.
2. Put letter squares into an opaque container such as a
   brown paper bag.
3. Pick a letter blindly from the bag.
4. Roll die.
5. Come up with a word (or words) that starts with the letter
   you picked and meets the following requirements according to the number you roll on the die:

   1 = one one-syllable word for one point
   2 = one two-syllable word for two points
   3 = one three-syllable word for three points
   4 = two two-syllable words, both beginning with the let-
       ter you picked, for four points or one four-syllable
       word for eight points
   5 = one two-syllable word and one three-syllable word,
       both beginning with the letter you picked, for five
       points or one five-syllable word for ten points
   6 = two three-syllable words, both beginning with the
       letter you picked, for six points or one six-syllable
       word for twelve points

6. No one may repeat a word previously named.
7. If you roll a four, five, or six and go for the two-word
   option, you must think of two appropriate words or you
   get no points for that turn.
8. Once you say a word, you are considered to have played
   it. For example, if you draw a *c* and roll a four and say
   "corruption," you get no points for that turn.
9. Proper names are not permitted.

10. Whoever is ahead when the timer goes off or whoever reaches one hundred points first wins.

Variations

1. If you find choosing squares inconvenient, take turns going through the alphabet. First player rolls die and gets a three, so he says "alphabet" for three points. Second player rolls die and gets a two, so he says "apple." First player rolls die, gets a six, and says "beautiful bicycle" for six points. Second player rolls die, gets a four, and says "behaviorist" for eight points, and so forth until both do z words. Whoever has the most points wins.

2. For younger, less verbal players, use a penny instead of a die. Heads means a player must come up with a one-syllable word, tails means a two-syllable word.

3. Games can be played with more than two persons.

Note

This game was inspired by a phenomenon that has intrigued psychologists: the tip-of-the-tongue phenomenon. When you know that you know a word but you just cannot put your mental finger on it, you are likely to say "I know it starts with a p and has three syllables." Roger Brown and David McNeill, psychologists who brought this phenomenon to our attention, comment that people in such a state "would appear to be in mild torment, something like the brink of a sneeze," and that if they find the word, their relief is likely to be considerable. The importance of the tip-of-the-tongue phenomenon to cognitive psychology is that it suggests that words are stored in our memories in terms of the way they sound as well as what they mean. I have had so many words stay on the tip of my tongue that I decided to make a game of the annoyance.

REPORTS

Purpose

To give your child familiarity with the idea of reports.

Game

Pick a topic about which you and your child know a fair amount. Take turns giving a different fact about that topic. Whoever cannot come up with a different fact or who makes a mistake must look up the topic in an encyclopedia, dictionary, or atlas.

Good topics might be: cats, dogs, rabbits, pine trees, violets, rain, rainbows, deserts, the state you live in, a state you have visited, apples, cars, circuses, rocks, the American Revolution.

To give you an idea of how the game is played, imagine that you first say, "Cats are mammals."

Your child responds: "Cats meow."

You say: "Cats have kittens."

Your child says: "Cats are related to tigers and lions."

You say: "Cats are domestic."

Your child says: "Cats have whiskers."

You say: "Cats have tails."

Your child says; "Wait a minute. Not all cats have tails. You lose."

You look up "cats" in the encyclopedia and find out about the Manx cat, which has no tail. You probably will find out some other new facts. On a different day, you and your child can try the same topic and see how much you remember from looking it up.

Variation

When your child has mastered the idea of reports, tackle the issue of organization. For example, with cats, each of you must name five facts about the appearance of cats (e.g., they have four legs, whiskers, fur, five claws on each paw, are felines, etc.). Then each names five facts about cats' habits (e.g., they eat meat, catch rats and birds, climb trees, purr, and meow). Finally, each names five aspects of cats' place in the animal kingdom, namely the biological classifications to which cats belong, and the different kinds of domestic cats possible (e.g., they are classified as *felis catus;* they are mammals; there are Persian, Himalayan, and Siamese cats, among other recognized breeds).

Again, when one of you comes up short on some subsection, you have to capitulate and look up the topic in an appropriate source.

Note

As was mentioned in the introduction to this section, your child will be spending a great deal of time at school learning to write reports during this stage of her life. It is one of the most important aspects of her education now. Playing an oral game that relates to what she is learning in school will help her master this new type of material and also make it an integral part of her life. What is learned and used solely at school often is tagged as boring or irrelevant, unfortunately. Also, you both will acquire a lot of in-formation in the process.

Bibliography

Achenbach, T. M. (1982). *Developmental psychopathology.* 2nd ed. New York: Wiley.

Ainsworth, M. D. S. (1973). The development of infant-mother attachment. In B. M. Caldwell & H. N. Ricciuti (eds.), *Review of child development research, Vol. 3* (pp. 1–94). Chicago: University of Chicago Press.

Ainsworth, M. D. S., & Bell, S. M. (1974). Mother-infant interaction and the development of competence. In K. J. Connolly & J. S. Bruner (eds.), *The growth of competence* (pp. 97–118). New York: Academic Press.

Barnes, S., Gutfreund, M., Satterly, D., & Wells, G. (1983). Characteristics of adult speech which predict children's language development. *Journal of Child Language, 10,* 65–84.

Bell, S. M., & Ainsworth, M. D. S. (1972). Infant crying and maternal responsiveness. *Child Development, 43,* 1171–1190.

Berko, J. (1958). The child's learning of English morphology. *Word, 14,* 150–177.

Bowlby, J. (1969). *Attachment.* New York: Basic Books.

Bretherton, I., McNew, S., Snyder, L., & Bates, E. (1983). Individual differences at 20 months: analytic and holistic strategies in language acquisition. *Journal of Child Language, 10,* 293–320.

Brown, R., & McNeill, D. (1966). The "tip of the tongue" phenomenon. *Journal of Verbal Learning and Verbal Behavior, 5,* 325–337.

237

Bruner, J. S. (1973). *Beyond the information given.* New York: Norton.

Bussis, A. M., Chittenden, E. A., Amarel, M., & Klausner, E. (1985). *Inquiry into meaning.* Hillsdale, N.J.: Erlbaum.

Cazden, C. B., Michaels, S., & Tabors, P. (1985). Self-repair in sharing time narrative: The intersection of metalinguistic awareness, speech event and narrative style. In S. W. Freedman (ed.), *The acquisition of written language: response and revision.* Norwood, N.J.: Ablex.

Chall, J. S. (1983). *Stages of reading development.* New York: McGraw-Hill.

Chomsky, N. (1957). *Aspects of the theory of syntax.* Cambridge, Mass.: M.I.T. Press.

Corte, M. D., Benedict, H., & Klein, D. (1983). The relationship of pragmatic dimensions of mothers' speech to the referential-expressive distinction. *Journal of Child Language, 10,* 35–43.

Eimas, P. D., Siqueland, E. R., Jusczyk, P., & Vigorito, J. (1971). Speech perception by infants. *Science, 171,* 303–306.

Elkind, D. (1981). *The hurried child.* Reading, Mass.: Addison-Wesley.

Erikson, E. H. (1977). *Toys and reasons.* New York: Norton.

Flavell, J. H. (1963). *The developmental psychology of Jean Piaget.* New York: D. Van Nostrand.

Furrow, D., Nelson, K., & Benedict, H. (1979). Mothers' speech to children and syntactic development: Some simple relationships. *Journal of Child Language, 6,* 423–442.

Furrow, D., & Nelson, K. (1984). Environmental correlates of individual differences in language acquisition. *Journal of Child Language, 11,* 523–534.

Gardner, H., Kircher, M., Winner, E., & Perkins, D. (1975). Children's metaphoric productions and preferences. *Journal of Child Language, 2,* 125–141.

Gibson, E. J., & Walk, R. D. (1960). The "visual cliff." *Scientific American, 202,* 64–72.

Gilligan, C. (1982). *In a different voice.* Cambridge, Mass.: Harvard University Press.

Gleason, J. B., & Greif, E. B. (1983). Men's speech to young children. In B. Thorne, C. Kramerae, & N. Henley (eds.), *Language, gender, and society.* Rowley, Mass.: Newbury House.

Gleason, J. B. (ed.) (1985). *The development of language.* Columbus, Ohio: Merrill.

Gleason, J. B. (1973). Code switching in children's language. In T. E. Moore (ed.), *Cognitive development and the acquisition of language.* New York: Academic Press.

Hemphill, L., & Siperstein, G. N. (1990). Conversational competence and peer response to mildly retarded children. *Journal of Educational Psychology, 82,* 128–134.

Irwin, O. C. (1949). Infant speech. *Scientific American, 181* (3), 22–24.

Istomina, Z. M. (1982). The development of voluntary memory in children of preschool age. In U. Neisser (ed.), *Memory observed.* San Francisco: W. H. Freeman.

Kail, R. (1979). *The development of memory in children.* San Francisco: W. H. Freeman.

Kohlberg, L. (1984). *The psychology of moral development: The nature and validity of moral stages.* San Francisco: Harper & Row.

Kuczaj, S. A. (1983). *Crib speech and language play.* New York: Springer-Verlag.

McCabe, A., & Peterson, C. (1985). A naturalistic study of the production of causal connectives by children. *Journal of Child Language, 12,* 145–159.

McCabe, A., & Peterson, C. (1984). What makes a good story? *Journal of Psycholinguistic Research, 13,* 457–480.

McCall, R. B., Appelbaum, M. I., & Hogarty, P. S. (1973). Developmental changes in mental performance. *Monographs of the Society for Research in Child Development, 38* (3, Serial No. 150).

Menig-Peterson, C., & McCabe, A. (1977–78). Children talk about death. *Omega, 8,* 305–317.

Nelson, K. E. (1973). Structure and strategy in learning to talk. *Monographs of the Society for Research in Child Development, 38* (Serial No. 149).

Nelson, K. E., Carskaddon, G., & Bonvillian, J. D. (1973). Syntax acquisition: Impact of experimental variation in adult verbal interaction with the child. *Child Development, 44,* 497–504.

Olsen-Fulero, L., & Conforti, J. (1983). Child responsiveness to mother questions of varying type and presentation. *Journal of Child Language, 10,* 495–520.

Peterson, C., & McCabe, A. (1985). Understanding "because": How important is the task? *Journal of Psycholinguistic Research, 14,* 199–218.

Peterson, C., & McCabe, A. (1983). *Developmental psycholinguistics: Three ways of looking at a child's narrative.* New York: Plenum Press.

Pollio, H. R., Barlow, J. M., Fine, H. J., & Pollio, M. R. (1977). *Psychology and the poetics of growth: Figurative language in psychology, psychotherapy, and education.* Hillsdale, N.J.: Erlbaum.

Reid, W. H. (1983). *Treatment of the DSM-III Psychiatric Disorders.* New York: Brunner/Mazel.

Rheingold, H. L., Gewirtz, J. L., & Ross, H. W. (1959). Social conditioning of vocalization in the infant. *Journal of Comparative Physiological Psychology, 52,* 68–73.

Roth, F. P. (1984). Accelerating language learning in young children. *Journal of Child Language, 11,* 89–108.

Sanders, E. K. (1972). When are speech sounds learned? *Journal of Speech and Hearing Disorders, 37,* 55–63.

Shantz, C. U., & Wilson, K. E. (1972). Training communication skills in young children. *Child Development, 43,* 693–698.

Smolak, L., & Weintraub, M. (1983). Maternal speech: Strategy or response? *Journal of Child Language, 10,* 369–380.

Snow, C. E. (1973). Mother's speech to language-learning children. *Child Development, 43,* 549–565.

Snow, C. E., & Ferguson, C. A. (eds.). (1977). *Talking to children: Language input and acquisition.* Cambridge: Cambridge University Press.

Snow, C. E., & Goldfield, B. A. (1983). Turn the page please: Situation-specific language acquisition. *Journal of Child Language, 10,* 551–570.

Snow, C. E., & Hoefnagel-Hohle, M. (1978). The critical period for language acquisition: Evidence from second language learning. *Child Development, 49*, 1114–1128.

Sullivan, J. W., & Horowitz, F. D. (1983). The effects of intonation on infant attention: The role of the rising intonation contour. *Journal of Child Language, 10*, 521–534.

Sulzby, E. (1986). Children's development of prosodic distinctions in telling and dictation modes. In A. Matsuhashi (ed.), *Writing in real time: Modeling production processes*. Norwood, N.J.: Ablex.

Weir, R. H. (1966). Some questions on the child's learning of phonology. In F. Smith & G. A. Miller (eds.), *The genesis of language*. Cambridge, Mass.: M.I.T. Press.

Werker, J. F., & Tees, R. C. (1984). Cross-language speech perception: Evidence for perceptual reorganization during the first year of life. *Infant Behavior and Development, 7*, 49–63.

Whitehurst, G. J., Falco, F. L., Lonigan, C. J., Fischel, J. E., DeBaryshe, B. D., Valdez-Menchaca, M. C., & Caulfield, M. (1988). Accelerating language development through picture reading. *Developmental Psychology, 24*, (4), 552–559.

Wittgenstein, L. (1953). *Philosophical investigations*, 3rd ed. New York: Macmillan.

ABOUT THE AUTHOR

ALLYSSA MCCABE, Ph.D., has taught at Southeastern Louisiana University and is currently teaching in the Department of Child Study at Tufts University and at the Harvard Graduate School of Education. Her work is widely published in professional journals such as *Developmental Psychology, Journal of Psycholinguistic Research,* and the *Journal of Child Language.* In addition, Dr. McCabe is the co-author, along with Carole Peterson, of *Developmental Psycholinguistics: Three Ways of Looking at a Child's Narrative* (Plenum Press) and *Developing Narrative Structure* (Erlbaum).

The mother of a young daughter and son, Dr. McCabe approaches the topic of language development as both a professional and a parent. She and her family live in Weston, Massachusetts.

Index